Power Searching the Internet

Power Searching the Internet

THE LIBRARIAN'S QUICK GUIDE

Nicole Hennig

 LIBRARIES
UNLIMITED™

An Imprint of ABC-CLIO, LLC

Santa Barbara, California • Denver, Colorado

Library of Congress Cataloging in Publication Control Number: 2018043995

ISBN: 978–1–4408–6697–5 (paperback)
    978–1–4408–6698–2 (ebook)

23 22 21 20 19   1 2 3 4 5

This book is also available as an eBook.

Libraries Unlimited
An Imprint of ABC-CLIO, LLC

ABC-CLIO, LLC
130 Cremona Drive, P.O. Box 1911
Santa Barbara, California 93116-1911
www.abc-clio.com

This book is printed on acid-free paper ∞

Manufactured in the United States of America

Google and the Google logo are registered trademarks of Google Inc., used with permission.

Contents

Introduction

Everyone knows how to dash off a quick Google search, but do you know how to go deeper when searching the internet? This book will show you how to search for many types of information effectively: websites, news, images, videos, statistics, maps, books, definitions, translations, and more. With examples and how-to tips, you'll learn to effectively search Google, social media sites, Wolfram Alpha, and other internet search tools.

Many people aren't familiar with advanced features and filtering options of search tools on the internet. This book will show you where to find those options and how to use them effectively. We'll cover the following:

- Using Google effectively.
- Using other Google sites: Google News, Google Translate, Google Books, Google Scholar, and Google Maps.
- Searching for images and videos.
- Social media searching of Twitter, Facebook, Instagram, and Pinterest.
- Finding old websites using the Wayback Machine and Google's cache.
- Searching for data, statistics, and comparisons, using Wolfram Alpha.

I'll summarize with some guidelines that apply to any internet search tool, ideas for using this guide for library instruction, and a list of resources for learning more.

After reading this book you will:

- Know how to search Google and other search engines more effectively.
- Know how to protect your privacy when searching.
- Be familiar with some of the hidden features and filters offered by search tools covered in this book.
- Know about several different free search tools and when to use each.
- Have information you can use to teach your patrons about searching.

One thing to keep in mind while reading this book is that features of internet search tools change frequently, so it's likely that some of the options I discuss in this book will have changed by the time you read this. However, the main concepts stay the same. I'll summarize those concepts in the final chapter.

I hope that you'll find these methods useful in all of your own searching and also when helping library users. Enjoy reading this book and becoming a power searcher!

Chapter 1

Using Google Effectively

Special Features

Search Predictions

When you dash off a quick Google search, one of the first things you notice is that Google begins to add words to what you type in a menu that appears below the search box. This is handy when it suggests words that you were planning to type anyway, or when you need suggestions for how you might phrase your search. (If you don't see any predictions, it's possible that the word you are searching for is too new or not popular enough to generate predictions.)

For example, if you type "solar powered air conditioner," it shows these options (and more) in a menu below the search box:

- solar powered air conditioner for rv
- solar powered air conditioner for car
- solar powered air conditioner for camping
- solar powered air conditioner window unit
- solar powered air conditioner unit
- solar powered air conditioner diy
- solar powered air conditioner apartment

Google calls these "search predictions." You might wonder how it generates these. According to Google's documentation, they are based on three things:

- What other people are searching for, including trending stories
- The content of web pages indexed by Google

- Your search history (if you are signed in to a Google account with web and app activity turned on)[1]

It's not possible to turn the suggestions off,[2] but you can ignore them. Sometimes they can be helpful because they suggest something that's relevant to you. You could also use them to do keyword research and see what words people are including with certain terms. It's also possible to find reputation management problems for particular brands. For example, try typing "crayola colored bubbles," and you'll see predictions for "class action lawsuit." Since your own recent searches might show up in the menu, it's useful to know that you can remove those from the menu by clicking "remove" next to the search phrase.

Google

bik	🎤
bike **accident tucson**	Remove
bik**ing trails in vermont**	Remove
bike **shop tucson**	
bik**ini**	
bike **shop**	
bike	

Sometimes you may see options that are racist or inappropriate in other ways since it's showing what many people search for and is a reflection of the society we live in. There is a link under the suggestions where you can "report inappropriate predictions."

If you follow that link, Google asks you which predictions were inappropriate and lists all of them with checkboxes for selecting them. They then give you a choice of saying whether they were hateful, sexually explicit, violent, dangerous and harmful activity, or other.

You might remember that before mid-2017 these predictions were called "autocomplete" and were in the search box itself, and appeared dynamically as you typed. In mid-2017 Google decided to move them into a drop-down menu because their data shows that more people are searching on mobile devices than computers, and

Which predictions were inappropriate?

☐ portable solar powered air conditioner

☐ diy solar powered air conditioner

☐ solar powered air conditioner for rv

☐ portable solar powered air conditioner camping

☐ solar powered air conditioner for car

☐ small solar powered air conditioner

☐ solar powered air conditioner for camping

☐ lennox solar powered air conditioner

The predictions selected above are:

○ Hateful

○ Sexually explicit

○ Violent

○ Dangerous and harmful activity

○ Other

Additional comments (optional)

Go to the Legal Help page to request content changes for legal reasons.

CANCEL   SEND

with a touchscreen, the menu works better than grayed-out letters in the search box.[3]

You can find many amusing instant predictions by entering a few words into the search box like these: "what is it called when," "what is the best," "what is the worst," "why do dogs," "why do cats," and so on.

Limiting and Sorting by Date

One of the most useful options of a Google search result is the ability to limit by date. Many people don't notice this feature because it's tucked away in a menu that's not apparent on the first screen. To find it, enter your search, and on the results screen look for a menu under the search box called "Tools," usually found on the far right of the screen. If you are on a mobile device, you will have to scroll the menu horizontally to see it.

When you select Tools, a submenu appears where the first choice is "Any Time," with a down arrow. Open that menu to see more choices like past hour, past 24 hours, past week, past month, past year, or a custom range.

This is very useful when the default results are a bit dated—such as when you are looking for help with a new technology. If you're finding pages that are too old, just limit to the current year or to a custom range, such as the past six months.

After you make your choice, such as "past month," you'll see another menu option next to it, where you can sort by date instead of by relevance. It's worth trying both types of sorting to see which one gives you the most relevant information for your search.

Verbatim Search

If you've ever felt frustrated because Google's results aren't including all of the words you entered, here is why. Google does the following to your default searches:

- Makes spelling corrections
- Gives preference to sites you've visited before
- Includes synonyms of your terms (like "car" when you searched "automotive")
- Finds results that match similar terms (like "floral delivery" when you searched "flower shops")

Verbatim searching didn't change the spelling of my term, "Carosel" to "Carousel" leading me to the restaurant I was looking for.

- Finds words with the same stem (like "running" when you typed "run")
- Makes some of your search terms optional

Google does this in an attempt to make natural language searching work well for you. Often this gives you good results, but sometimes it doesn't. In those cases, you can use Google's "verbatim" search.

To find it, enter your search terms, and on the results screen look for the "Tools" menu on the far right. Select it and you'll see a sub menu that includes the date filters discussed previously. Next to that is a menu that says, "All Results." Select that to switch to "Verbatim." Now your results won't be influenced by the items mentioned above.[4]

Advanced Search Features

Google Advanced Search has several features worth knowing about. You can find the advanced screen by looking in the Settings menu for "Advanced Search," either on Google's home page or on your results screen.

The first few choices are "Find pages with. . ."

- All of these words
- This exact word or phrase
- Any of these words
- None of these words

One thing to keep in mind is that even when you use these features, Google still follows its practices mentioned in the previous section, such as making some of your search terms optional or finding words with the same stem. For example, if you were to enter the following terms into the box marked "all of these words," — **amazon echo public library**—you would get some results that don't include every word, such as a story about Amazon Echo in a school library (missing "public") or a book on Amazon about public libraries (missing "echo").

To make sure all of your terms are included, use the verbatim search, described in the previous section. You can also use quotes around a single term to make sure it is included in your results. If you ever see "**missing:term | must include:term**" under a result, you can click the link on the term itself, after "must include." This will put pages containing that word back into your results set.

Different Motivations for Different Generations of Workers: Boomers ...
https://www.inc.com/.../different-motivations-for-different-generations-of-workers-boo...
Oct 17, 2017 - Different Motivations for Different **Generations** of Workers: Boomers, Gen X, **Millennials**,
and Gen Z.
Missing: ~~perennials~~ | Must include: perennials

New Perspectives: Forget Millennials, target Perennials – Zenith
https://www.zenithmedia.com/new-perspectives-forget-millennials-target-perennials/ ▾
Dec 14, 2017 - **Perennials** are not defined by age but by mindset. Yet although Pell is clear that this
group crosses **generations** and is more categorized by attitude than age, the ...

That said, it can still be useful to use these fields, especially since they remind you of which operators you can use on the main Google screen. You can type the minus sign to exclude words, the Boolean operator "OR" to show any of the words, and use quotes around your terms to find exact phrases. The plus sign as a way to indicate required terms was discontinued in 2011,[5] but you can use quotes around a single term to make sure it is included in your results.

For example, if you're searching for information about the safety of Elon Musk's invention called the Hyperloop, you could use the advanced screen. Enter **hyperloop** in "all of these words" and enter **safety crash terrorism** in "any of these words." On the results screen Google enters your search in the box like this: **hyperloop safety OR crash OR terrorism**.

This is helpful for reminding you how Google works, so you can use these operators on the main screen. What's more helpful is to realize that Google doesn't act like library databases and isn't designed for this type of precision searching. Google instead is focused on natural language searching. It often works best to enter your query as a question that you might ask aloud during a conversation. For example, you could enter phrases like "**how high is the tokyo sky tree**" or "**what is the tallest building in the world**." (Question marks aren't needed). Since many people search on mobile devices these days, and many use the microphone to speak their search into their phone, Google aims to provide answers quickly and directly to these queries.[6] And now with the rise of smart digital assistants like Amazon Alexa, Google Home, and Siri, we see even more effort to improve natural language searching by Google. Google does this in its Google Assistant app, designed for voice searching on mobile phones or with the Google Home smart speaker.[7]

Advanced Search: Narrowing Options

The most useful parts of the advanced search screen are the narrowing options. With these, you can limit by geographic region, limit by language, limit by site or domain, limit by file type, and search for terms that appear in specific parts of a page, such as in the title or in links to a page.

Then narrow your
results by...

language:	any language
region:	any region
last update:	anytime
site or domain:	
terms appearing:	anywhere in the page
SafeSearch:	Show most relevant results
file type:	any format
usage rights:	not filtered by license

Limit by Language

Let's look at some examples of how limits work. Limiting by language is useful when you want to read content in a language other than your first language. Search for "Frida Kahlo" and limit to Spanish to read articles about her in Spanish. If you want to use Google entirely in Spanish, you can visit the Settings screen and select Language, then select Español from the choices there. Be sure to save your selection. Google reminds you that saved choices are available whenever you are signed in to Google.

Be sure to select "show more" to see all of the languages available. Google is adding more languages all the time. For fun, try changing your settings to one of the silly language choices that Google has added as jokes, such as Elmer Fudd, or Hacker. Don't worry, it's easy to change it back to English or whatever language you prefer.

Limit by Region

Another useful feature is the "limit by region" choice. Let's say you are searching for information about a place called the Riverside Bridge. That is a very common name, found in places all over the

Search Settings

Search results	**Which language should Google products use?**
Languages	
Help	

○ Deutsch ◉ English ○ español ○ español (Latinoamérica) ○ français

○ hrvatski ○ italiano ○ Nederlands ○ polski ○ português (Brasil)

○ português (Portugal) ○ Tiếng Việt ○ Türkçe ○ русский ○ العربية

○ ไทย ○ 한국어 ○ 中文 (简体) ○ 中文 (繁體) ○ 日本語

○ Acoli ○ Afrikaans ○ Akan ○ azərbaycan ○ Balinese ○ Bork, bork, bork! ○ bosanski ○ brezhoneg ○ català ○ Cebuano ○ čeština ○ chiShona ○ Corsican ○ Cymraeg ○ dansk ○ Èdè Yorùbá ○ eesti ○ Elmer Fudd ○ esperanto ○ euskara ○ Eʋegbe

○ Ichibemba ○ Igbo ○ Ikirundi ○ Indonesia ○ Interlingua ○ isiZulu ○ íslenska ○ Javanese ○ Kinyarwanda ○ Kiswahili ○ Klingon ○ Kongo ○ kreol morisien ○ Krio (Sierra Leone) ○ Latin ○ latviešu ○ lea fakatonga ○ lietuvių ○ lingála ○ Lozi ○ Luba-Lulua

○ Occitan ○ Oromoo ○ Pirate ○ română ○ rumantsch ○ Runasimi ○ Runyankore ○ Seychellois Creole ○ shqip ○ Sindhi ○ slovenčina ○ slovenščina ○ Soomaali ○ Southern Sotho ○ srpski (Crna Gora) ○ srpski (latinica) ○ Sundanese ○ suomi ○ svenska ○ Tswana ○ Tumbuka

○ татар ○ тоҷикӣ ○ українська ○ ქართული ○ Հայերեն ○ ייִדיש ○ עברית ○ نوێغۆرچه ○ اردو ○ پنتو ○ فارسی ○ کوردیی ناوەندی ○ ትግርኛ ○ አማርኛ ○ नेपाली ○ मराठी ○ हिन्दी ○ বাংলা ○ ਪੰਜਾਬੀ ○ ગુજરાતી ○ ଓଡ଼ିଆ

Google

Google Seawch   I'm Feewing Wucky

Google offered in: English

Google with language settings changed to "Elmer Fudd"

world. Often Google will use your current location and find places close to you with that name. But if you're searching for a place that's not nearby, it's useful to limit by region. If you are in the United States but looking for a Riverside Bridge in the United Kingdom, you can limit by that region and quickly find the one you are looking for.

Limit by Site or Domain

Let's begin with an example in order to see the usefulness of this next option. Suppose you are looking for varying opinions of the "UnCollege movement." As a basic Google search, you might simply type **opinions of the uncollege movement**. When I tried this search, the results on the first screen were mostly from ".com" sites, with a few ".org" sites.

If you switch to the advanced search screen and limit your search to site or domain:edu, you will get results only from pages hosted by educational institutions. Results from those institutions might have very different opinions of the UnCollege movement than what you found in your initial search. It will also help bring those sites to the first few screens of results, instead of buried deep within your initial result set.

If the difference between a site and a domain is not fresh in your mind, here is a reminder. For example, "stanford.edu" is the *domain* for Stanford University, and "explorecourses.stanford.edu," is a *site* at Stanford. Sites can also take this form, "stanford.edu/news." This is a useful feature to use when a particular site doesn't have a useful or easily findable search engine of its own.

It's useful to know the most common top-level domain extensions and what they are used for. In the 1980s, seven top-level domain extensions were created.[8] These first three are unrestricted (anyone can use them), but were originally intended for commercial businesses, internet service providers, and noncommercial organizations respectively.

- .com (commercial)
- .net (network)
- .org (noncommercial organization)

These next four are restricted to particular types of groups.[9]

- .int (international)
- .mil (military)
- .edu (education)
- .gov (government)

In addition, there are two-letter country code domain extensions for websites from particular countries. It's not required to use these, so many places use .com, .edu, or .org instead, but many governmental organizations use them. So they can be a handy way to search for information on government websites from a particular country.

Here are a few examples:

- .ca (Canada)
- .cn (mainland China)
- .fr (France)
- .ch (Switzerland)
- .au (Australia)
- .in (India)
- .de (Germany)
- .jp (Japan)

You can find a complete list of these on the wiki of ICANN (Internet Corporation for Assigned Names and Numbers), https://icannwiki.org/Country_code_top-level_domain. ICANN was formed in 1998 and is a nonprofit partnership of people from around the world who work to coordinate unique identifiers for the internet.

Since the 1980s, many more domain extensions have been added, such as the following:

- .biz
- .info
- .jobs
- .mobi
- .name

You can view a huge list of all of these on the website of IANA (Internet Assigned Numbers Authority), https://www.iana.org/domains/root/db.

Some domain extensions aren't actually used for what they were originally designed for. One example is the .co country code for Colombia. Some companies use it since it can also stand for "company." For an example, see the digital agency Two Words (https://twowords.co). Others use two-letter country codes as part of creative domain names like about.me, bit.ly, last.fm, postach.io, or thanksforteaching.us.

So when you are filtering by domain, you'll probably get the best results for *most* queries using the seven original domain extensions mentioned above, since that's what most sites use.

Where Terms Appear

Another useful option on the advanced search screen is called "terms appearing." In this menu you can select from:

- Anywhere in the page
- In the title of the page
- In the text of the page
- In the URL of the page
- In links to the page

Searching for words in the title of a page is useful when your results contain pages that *mention* your terms but aren't primarily *about* the topic. Switch your search to the advanced screen and select "in the title of the page" for better results. It's likely that if your terms are in the title, the page is about that topic.

Another useful option is to search for terms that appear "in links to the page." With this, you can find out which other pages are linking to pages on your own site (or any site). You will often find pages from the site itself first since most sites have many internal links to their own pages, but if you scroll past those, you'll find other sites that link to the page in question. If you are the webmaster of a site, you can use Google webmaster tools to see links to your site: https://www.google.com/webmasters/tools. There are also other tools for finding links to your site or any site. These are known as "backlink checkers." Two of my favorites are Open Site Explorer, https://moz.com/link-explorer, and Link Explorer, http://www.openlinkprofiler.org. With these you can enter a URL in the box and get a list of pages that link to that page.

Limit by File Type

One more useful option on the advanced search screen is "limit by file type." In this menu you can select from the following types:

- Adobe Acrobat PDF (.pdf)
- Adobe Postscript (.ps)
- Autodesk DWF (.dwf)
- Google Earth KML (.kml)
- Google Earth KML (.kmz)
- Microsoft Excel (.xls)
- Microsoft Powerpoint (.ppt)
- Microsoft Word (.doc)
- Rich Text Format (.rtf)
- Shockwave Flash (.swf)

Let's say you are searching for trend reports about new technologies. In the first search box enter **technology trend report 2018**, and then select PDF from the file type menu.

Since many trend reports are available for free online as PDFs, this gives you a useful list to choose from. When I did this search, I found useful reports from Accenture, Deloitte, and Future Today Institute. You could look for many types of free reports this way.

---

technology trend report 2018 filetype:pdf   🎤   🔍

All   News   Images   Videos   Shopping   More   Settings   Tools

---

About 19,700,000 results (0.43 seconds)

New technology trends 2018 | Complimentary Gartner Report
[Ad] www.insight.com/ ▾
Download Your Complimentary Gartner **2018 Technology Trends Report** Today! Unique Strategies. In Business Since 1988.
Small Business Solutions · Cloud & Data Center · Supply Chain Optimization

[PDF] Accenture Technology Vision 2018 – Tech Trends Report
https://www.accenture.com/t20180227T215953Z.../tech...2018/.../Accenture-TechVisi... ▾
Feb 23, 2018 - We invite you to explore the Accenture **Technology**. Vision **2018**, our annual forecast of the **technology trends** unfolding in the next three years.

[PDF] Tech Trends 2018 - Deloitte
https://www2.deloitte.com/.../Tech-Trends-2018/4109_TechTrends-2018_FINAL.pdf
Oct 30, 2017 - The theme of this year's **Tech Trends report** is the symphonic enterprise, an idea that describes ... **Tech** Trends **2018**: The symphonic enterprise.

[PDF] 2018 Tech Trends - Helt Digital
https://helt.digital/wp-content/uploads/2017/10/ONA-Trends_7.pdf ▾
tech trends report specifically for the future of journalism. .... The Future Today Institute's **2018 Tech** Trends For Journalism Report is our first industry-specific.

Finding Similar Sites

Another Google search feature that can be useful is the "related" operator. It's not found on the advanced screen, so you need to remember how to use it. It's designed to find sites that are similar to or related to another site.

To use it, enter **related:** and then the URL (without http) of the site you want to find related sites for. For example, let's say you want to find nonprofit organizations that are similar to the Electronic Frontier Foundation (eff.org). On the main Google search screen, enter **related:eff.org**. There should be *no space* between the colon and the URL. The results include similar nonprofits, such as the Center for Democracy and Technology, American Civil Liberties Union, and the Center for Constitutional Rights. This doesn't work for every type of search, but when it does work, it's useful.

Using Advanced Features on the Main Google Screen with Operators

One useful thing about the advanced search screen is that it reminds you of the exact syntax to use, should you prefer to use operators on the main search screen.

With the file type limit example above, the results screen will show the search box filled in with this: **technology trend report 2018 filetype:pdf**. And with the "limit by site" example, you'll see this: **opinions of the uncollege movement site:edu**. With all of these operators, you'll need to make sure there is no space after the colon and before your terms. Enter your search on the main Google screen and follow it by one of these limiting operators and a colon, then your selection. This can save you time for searches you do frequently.

To see a list of these operators, see Google's help page called "Refine Web Searches," https://tinyurl.com/ydhdjy7d.

Personalization

Search Results from Your Google Products

If you use Google products like Google Calendar, Google Contacts, Google Photos, or Gmail, you can search all of your content from those using the Google search engine. To do this, you need to be logged into your Google account in the browser you are using.

Do a search, and then switch to the tab called **Personal**. You can find this under the **More** option.

For example, I searched for Amtrak, then selected the **Personal** tab. On the results screen, Google showed me the phone number for Amtrak since I had it stored in my Google Contacts. It also showed me my Amtrak Guest Rewards membership number (found in my Gmail). It then showed me email messages from Amtrak (from Gmail), and my browsing history (previous searches for Amtrak information).

This can be useful if you use Google products. You can use Google to search across all of them. For each type of result, Google reminds you that "only you can see this result." If you prefer not to get these personal results, you can turn this off in the settings. Go to the Settings menu, choose Search Settings, and then look for Private Results. Switch to "do not use private results."

Private results

Private results help find more relevant content for you, including content and connections that only you can see.

◉ Use private results

◯ Do not use private results

Useful Operators for Personal Results

Google offers some useful operators for searching for your personal information. You can enter any of these on the main Google search screen:

- My events
- My bills
- My packages
- My reservations
- My flights
- My photos

Google will search across all of your Google products (most of these can be found in your Gmail), and show you results that only you can see.

For example, if you search for **my packages**, it will show you a list of shipping notices from your Gmail. For each, you can click on a down arrow to get more information about each package.

Most of these options only show items coming up in the future (flights, events, etc.), but some of them also offer an option to see past items. "My flights" shows an option called "past flights." If you don't have flights coming up, you can enter **my past flights** on the main Google screen.

If you use Google Photos, there are some useful ways to refine your search. On the main Google screen, you can enter **my photos**. You can also try entering places or years, such as **my photos Budapest**, or **my photos 2017**.

my packages   🎤   🔍

All   Maps   Shopping   Books   News   More   Settings   Tools

About 1,050,000,000 results (0.54 seconds)

Your purchases
Only you can see these results

Partially shipped · Northeastern Products...

Amazon
Partially shipped · Read This if You Want to Be...

Amazon
Completed · Find It Fast: Extracting Expert Information from Social Networks, Big...

Amazon
Shipped · Shoe Rack Storage Bench..., ClosetMaid 3456 Large...

To learn more about these options, see Google's help page, "Search Results from Your Google Products," https://support.google.com/websearch/answer/1710607.

How Google Personalizes Your Results

Even if you don't use Google products, there are other ways that Google personalizes your results. The following items influence your search results:

- Your location
- Your search history
- Your web browsing history
- Your Google+ account

Google began this practice in 2005, but only for people who were logged into Google accounts while they searched. In 2009, they rolled it out to everyone, even those who are not logged in. They track your web browsing and search history using cookies (small bits of text that sites use to track information for repeat visits, such as your username). So if you use the same computer repeatedly, without deleting your cookies or history, Google has a record of what you've searched and pages you've visited. If you use Google on a mobile device (or give it permission to know your location on your computer), there is also location history that is used to personalize your results.

It is possible to turn this off in your settings, telling Google not to save your history or searches. I'll show you how to do this in the next section, on privacy. For now, I'd like to show you examples of how this influences your searches while it's turned on.

Let's say you enter **biking trails**. Google will use your location to show you results about biking trails near you. If you are on a desktop or laptop without location turned on, Google uses the IP address of your internet connection to guess your approximate location. I'm currently living in Tucson, Arizona, so when I search for biking trails I see a list of 25 bike trails at the top of my results (there are many in the Tucson area). Below that, Google shows a map of Tucson with listings for local bike rental shops, bike tour companies, and bike repair shops. Below that are the usual Google results. All of them on the first page are for biking trail information in the Tucson area. If I wanted to find biking trails for other areas, I could simply enter **biking trails in Vermont**, or something similar.

---

biking trails	🎤 🔍

All   Maps   Images   Videos   News   More   Settings   Tools

About 97,000,000 results (0.63 seconds)

25 bike trails

Trail Name	City	Length
Snakedance Loop	Tucson	8
Sweetwater Preserve	Tucson	10
Tortolita Preserve	Tucson	9
Tucson Mountain Park	Tucson	1

26 more rows

Tucson, AZ Mountain Bike Trails | Mountain biking ... - Singletracks.com
https://www.singletracks.com/Mountain-Bike-Trails-bike-trails_0.html?filterBy=|loc...

The reason that Google makes search and browsing history influence your results is that they want to make it easier to find things that you search for frequently. For example, if you enter **kafka** because you are searching for Apache Kafka, an open-source stream-processing software platform, Google may remember that and put those results higher than results about the author Franz Kafka. Of course, you can always be more specific, and enter **apache kafka** or **franz kafka**, depending on what you're searching for.

If you have a Google+ account, and you are logged into Google while searching, Google will give a higher ranking to posts from people you are connected with there. So if you are searching for reviews of a particular movie and one of your Google+ contacts has posted about it, you'll very likely see their post on your first screen of results.

The important thing to remember about Google's personalization is that results will vary depending on where you are, who you are, which computer or mobile device you're using, and what privacy features you have enabled. Sometimes this gives you more relevant results, and sometimes it doesn't. In the next section, we'll look at several ways to control your privacy and not see personalized results.

Privacy of Your Google Data

Your Search and Web Browsing History

If you don't like the idea of Google saving all of your search and browsing history, there is a way to tell them to stop saving it. There is also a way to delete your previous search history, all at once, or for particular searches.

To find these options, go to Settings, then Search Settings. This is available on the desktop site, not the Google mobile app or mobile site. Look for the section called **Search History**. Follow the "search history" link there and you'll find your "My Activity" page: https://myactivity.google.com/. This page can be accessed directly on desktop or mobile sites. This is a page that only *you* can see, while you're signed in to Google.

If you've never looked at your "My Activity" page, you might be surprised to see how much information Google has about all of your activity. It includes all of your search and browsing history (desktop and mobile), pages you visited while using the Chrome browser, all of your Google Maps searches, your voice and audio activity (if you have a Google Home smart speaker or if you search by voice in Google's app or website), your Google Assistant activity (if you use the app on your mobile device or if it powers your Google Home speaker or Chromecast device), and your use of Google's products like Google News, Google Play Music, YouTube, the Google Play Store, and more.

It Can Be Useful to Search Your Own History

You can browse through your recent activity, or you can search all of it. In the search box at the top, enter your terms, then choose filters for product and date range. For example, if you enter nothing in the search box, select YouTube from the list of products, and select last 30 days from the dates menu, you'll see a list of everything you searched for and watched on YouTube in the last 30 days. This is handy if you are looking for something you saw but can't quite remember the name of.

How to Stop Saving History

You can tell Google to stop saving your activity for each product separately by using the choices on the top of this page: https://myaccount.google.com/activitycontrols. You can also find it in the upper left menu, under "activity controls."

On this page you'll see a section for each type of activity, beginning with "Web & App Activity." You can turn off each one by changing the button that is on by default for everything. Scroll down to see different types of activity, such as your YouTube watch history and more.

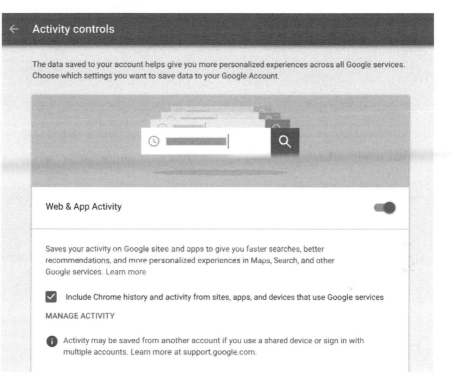

How to Delete Your History

Another option in Google's menus on this page is "Delete activity by." Select this and you'll find a screen with options for deleting particular activity. You can select a date, a date range, and a product or products, in order to give Google specific instructions for what to delete. One of the date choices is "all time," in case you want to delete all of your history for everything or for particular Google products. Google products listed here include the following:

- Ads
- Assistants
- Books
- Chrome
- Developers
- Express
- Gmail
- Google Apps
- Google News
- Google Play Books
- Google Play Store
- Google ⸍

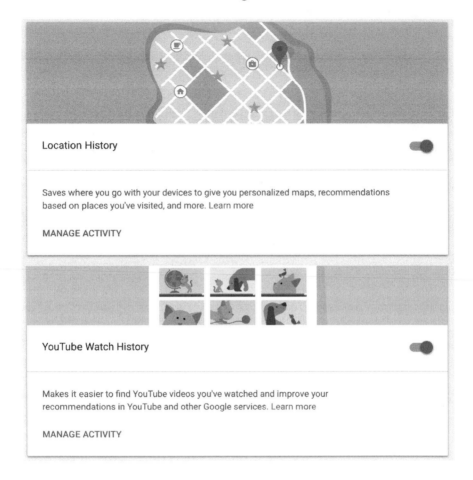

- Help
- Image Search
- Maps
- News
- Play Music
- Search
- Shopping
- Trips
- Video Search
- Voice and Audio
- YouTube

You can see that it's quite a comprehensive list of products — and it's easy to forget how many of the services you use are part of Google.

Advantages and Disadvantages of Deleting Your Google History   You may want to delete your history if you are being investigated by

← **Delete activity by**

Delete by topic or product

Search by keyword or filter by product, then select Delete results from the more options ⋮ menu, to delete all matching activity

TRY IT

Delete by date

Today   ▼

After June 21   ▼   Before June 21   ▼

All products   ▼

DELETE

police or federal investigators or if you just don't like the idea of Google storing all of your private data. Police and other investigators often request user data from Google, but they need to have a search warrant to get your search history from them. Google publishes statistics on how many requests they receive and fulfill in their "Transparency Report," found at https://transparencyreport .google.com. Recent figures (January through June 2017), show that Google received 48,941 requests for data from 83,345 accounts and produced user information for 65 percent of them. These numbers have been increasing over the past few years. Learn more about this in "Google Warns That Govt Is Demanding More of Your Private Data than Ever," by Liam Tung, September 29, 2017, ZDNet, https://www.zdnet.com/article/ google-warns-that-govt-is-demanding-more-of-your-private-data -than-ever.

On the other hand, if you delete and stop saving your history, you won't benefit from the customization that Google provides by looking at your history and location. They use your data in several ways, such as recommending YouTube videos you might want to watch, autocompleting your searches, customizing your Google Maps for getting directions to particular places, and auto-filling forms with your name, email, and other data. You can learn more on Google's Privacy Page, found at https://privacy.google.com/ your-data.html.

If you are considering the option of deleting all or some of your history, you might want to consider downloading everything Google has about you first. To do this, visit https://takeout.google.com.

There is quite a comprehensive list of data on that page, and you may want to download it from time to time even if you aren't planning on deleting your history. It could be useful to examine your own data or export it to other services (such as for importing your Google Contacts into another address book). This Takeout service includes all of your activity, and also data like your bookmarks, Google Pay data, Hangouts, Google Voice, Google Play Books, and more. You can select individual items or everything. You can choose what file type to save it as and how to receive it: with a download link via email, add to Google Drive, add to Dropbox, or add to Microsoft OneDrive. Google reminds you that it could take a few minutes or several hours, depending on the size of your archive. For more details, see Google's help page called "Download Your Data," https://support.google .com/accounts/answer/3024190?hl=en.

Private Browsing Mode

If you don't mind keeping your history turned on (so you can search your past sessions), you might find it convenient to use private browsing mode from time to time for particular searches.

Most web browsers have a choice in the menu called "New private window," or "New incognito window." When you use a private window, the following items won't be saved:

- Browsing history
- Cookies
- Information you enter in forms

This is useful when you don't want to leave a history for others who share your computer (at home or on public computers). However, the pages you browse will still be visible to your internet service provider or the owner of the computer's network (such as your school or employer). This is because network administrators keep statistics on usage, gathering lists of what pages are visited by every computer on the network. In addition, the individual websites that you visit very likely keep statistics on which computers visit their pages (by saving your IP address).

So remember that private browsing is only private from others who share your computer (and could view your history), not from websites, Google, or network administrators. In order to be truly private, see the next section, where I recommend specific tools for this purpose.

Other Privacy Tools

If you would like to browse and search privately, there are a few tools that I'd like to recommend.

The first is a search engine called DuckDuckGo. Their slogan is "The search engine that doesn't track you." They don't store any of your personal information or track you for advertising. You can visit their page using any browser on desktop or mobile at https://duckduckgo.com. They also have a mobile app for either iOS or Android; see https://duckduckgo.com/app. They have many of the same advanced searching features that Google has. See their help pages for more information: https://duck.co/help/results/syntax.

Another search engine that makes it their mission to protect privacy is StartPage, https://www.startpage.com. They also have mobile apps and many of the same features as DuckDuckGo. If you're interested in reading a detailed comparison of these two private search tools, see "DuckDuckGo or Startpage—Update (March 2, 2017)," Security Spread, http://securityspread.com/2016/10/24/duckduckgo-startpage-2016-update.

One more useful tool for private browsing is a mobile app called Firefox Focus (iOS and Android), https://www.mozilla.org/en-US/firefox/mobile/. This free app is set up by default with privacy protection. It doesn't track your history or allow ad trackers. I don't use this as the primary browser on my phone because it doesn't have features I rely on like bookmarking or tabs. But for the occasional search that I want to keep private, it's useful.

Stronger Privacy Using a VPN (Virtual Private Network)

Remember that even with these privacy tools, your internet service provider (or employer or school network administrator) can see which sites you visit. If you want to make your activity private from them, a good solution is to use a VPN service. These services encrypt all of your traffic between your computer or mobile device and the sites you visit, so it can't be seen by anyone.[10] VPNs are available for desktop and mobile platforms and are simple to use—you just turn the VPN on with one click and keep it running while using your device.

There are many VPN apps available. It's worth paying for one since some of the free ones aren't legitimate and don't work well. My

VPN of choice is ExpressVPN, https://www.expressvpn.com, for which I pay $8.32 per month (with a yearly subscription). For advice on how to choose a VPN, see "Choosing the VPN That's Right for You," by the Electronic Frontier Foundation, https://ssd.eff.org/en/module/choosing-vpn-thats-right-you.

Chapter 2

Using Other Google Sites Effectively

It's worth knowing some tips about using Google's other sites, like News, Translate, Books, Scholar, and Maps. This section focuses on some features that you might not remember or notice if you only use these from time to time.

Google News

Let's begin with Google News. You can use the Google News mobile app for iOS or Android, or on the website: https://news.google.com/. On the website, you'll see Top Stories first, with a sidebar that includes subcategories, like U.S., World, Local, Business, Technology, and so on. If you aren't signed in to a Google account, Google uses the IP address of your internet connection to guess at your approximate location. That way it can customize local news for your area and show you top stories for your country.

Customizing Topics, Locations, and Sources

It's useful to sign in to a Google account because then you can customize and save your options. You can view each broad category and choose to follow it by clicking the link marked "Follow" with a star next to it. When you click on the Favorites section in the sidebar, you'll see the topics you've followed, such as Business or

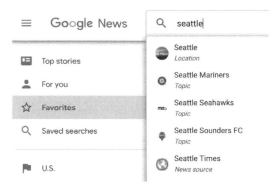

Technology. If you want to follow only certain subcategories, you can select those instead of the broad one.

In the Favorites section, you can also save Locations. This is useful if you want to regularly get news from locations beyond where you are currently. To add locations, use the search bar at the top, and when you begin to type a city name (such as Seattle) before you hit enter you'll see a drop-down menu of locations, sources, and topics that begin with that name. Select the option marked "Location." When you're on that screen you can favorite it as a location, just as you do for topics.

You can also mark certain sources as favorites. Search for a source, such as The Atlantic, and before you hit enter, look for "News source" under its name. Go to that page and mark it as a favorite.

Saving Searches

Another useful feature of Google News is the ability to save searches. So if you find yourself searching for certain types of news regularly, this is helpful. For example, I searched for the phrase "digital nomads" (using quotes to force an exact phrase search). On the results screen I clicked on "Save" (with a star next to it), and now it appears in my Saved Searches (linked in the sidebar).

Always Look in the "Three Dots" Menu

Another way to customize your results is to hide stories from particular sources. When you are browsing headlines in your results, there are some useful options under each headline. You'll see the source name (such as Washington Post), the date, a save icon, a share icon, and a three dots icon. The three small dots are sometimes hard to see, but the icon contains useful functions. (If you are using the Google News mobile app, the dots are more prominent.)

After selecting the three dots (on desktop browsers), you'll see these options:

- View full coverage
- Hide stories from [source name]

- More stories like this
- Fewer stories like this

The mobile app contains additional options under the three dots icon: save for later, share, go to [source name].

Behind Most Wildfires, a Person and a Spark: 'We Bring Fire With Us'
The New York Times · today

- As wildfire costs reach new heig
  homeowners get socked on insu
  East Bay Times · today

World

Families in North and Sout
reunited for first time since Korean War

View full coverage

Go to The New York Times

Hide all stories from The New York Times

More stories like this

Fewer stories like this

If you don't want to see stories from particular sources, you can hide the source from this menu. To see what you've hidden, look in Settings, Hidden Sources. You can reverse your choice by clicking Manage in that section. You can also select "more stories like this" (thumbs up icon) or the opposite, to train Google according to your preferences.

View Full Coverage—A Useful Aggregation

One of the most useful features of Google News is the ability to see an overview of how stories are being covered by different sources. They have made this easy to do with an option called "View Full Coverage." You can find this in several places. One is at the bottom of the first section of Top Headlines. Another is on individual head lines, in the "three dots" menu.

When you select View Full Coverage, you'll see an aggregation of news from different sources, including Top Coverage, videos, a timeline, recent updates from Twitter, and All Coverage.

For example, when searching for stories about the legalization of marijuana in Canada, you'll see stories from sources as diverse as *High Times, Weed Reader, The Denver Post,* and *The Globe and Mail,* next to each other.

Timeline

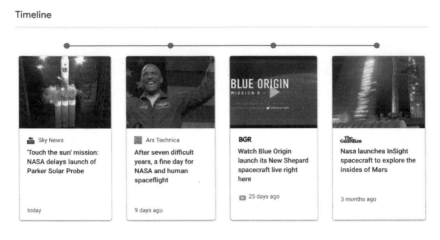

An example of a timeline from the full coverage feature in Google News.

Filters for Google News Searching

To see some useful filters in Google News, start your search at google.com. On your results screen, switch to the News tab. From there you'll see a Tools menu on the right side of the screen. Click that to see three submenus.

The first menu allows you to switch from the "all news" default to blogs. This is useful for seeing news from some smaller sources that may not appear in the first few screens of All News.

The next menu allows you to filter by date, with the following choices:

- Past hour
- Past 24 hours
- Past week
- Past month
- Past year
- Archives
- Custom range . . .

This is of course very useful when you're looking for breaking news on a topic and also for past news stories from particular dates.

The third menu lets you switch from "sorted by relevance" to "sorted by date," bringing the newest stories to the top.

If Google has changed how these features work by the time you read this, don't worry. The main point is to always look for menus where you can filter your results in useful ways. Also, use the customization features if you frequently want to browse Google News.

What Sources End Up in Google News?

You might wonder how Google News decides what is "top news" and how it ranks stories. It's worth reading Google's documentation on this, found in their Producer Help Center, https://tinyurl .com/yavyuyax. Here's what they say about ranking:

> In general, Google News aims to promote original journalism, as well as to expose users to diverse perspectives. Ranking in Google News is determined algorithmically based on a number of factors, including:

- Freshness of content
- Diversity of content
- Rich textual content
- Originality of content.

The most useful sections of Google's Producer Help for understanding Google's scope are "Content Policies," "Curation on Google News," and "Ranking."

Google Translate

If you ever need to translate text between languages, Google Translate can be helpful. It's not perfect, but has improved a lot in recent years and is especially helpful on your mobile phone when traveling to a country where you don't speak the language. It supports over 100 languages. You can use it on your desktop browser at https://translate.google.com, and also as a mobile app for iOS or Android (https://translate.google.com/intl/en/about/).

Voice Input on Desktop and Mobile

The most obvious way to begin (in your desktop browser) is to type some text in one language, choose a language in the second box for it to be translated to, and click Translate. Did you know that you can also turn on speech input? Just click the small microphone icon, allow access to your computer's microphone, and then speak. You can also click the speaker icon to hear the translated phrase spoken. This is the obvious way to use it in the mobile app, but it can also be convenient to use it that way on your desktop or laptop.

Google

Translate   Turn off instant trans

| English | Spanish | French | Detect language | ▾ |

Korean | Norwegian | Spanish | ▾ | **Translate**

hello how are you   ×

안녕하세요, 당신은 어떠세요?

17/5000

annyeonghaseyo, dangsin-eun eotteoseyo?

Speak Now

how, hello

Enter a URL or Upload a Document

In addition to typing or speaking text into the box, you can also enter the URL of a web page in order to translate it. For example, I copied and pasted the URL of the homepage for the Frida Kahlo Museum in Mexico City into the box (http://www.museofridakahlo.org .mx/esp/1/el-museo/la-casa/la-casa-azul), and selected a translation from Spanish to English. Google displayed a copy of the entire page, translated into English. You can also upload a document from your computer (such as a Word document or PDF), by clicking "translate a document" found under the first input box. After a few seconds, Google will display the entire document, in the new language.

Using Translate from the Main Google Screen

You can also use Google Translate from the main Google search screen. Here is an example. I was living in Budapest for a few months in 2015 and I don't speak Hungarian. I wanted to buy some dill for a dip I was making, and I needed to know the Hungarian word for it, so I could recognize labels in the grocery store. At Google's main search box, I entered **translate dill to Hungarian**. This works well as a quick way to translate single words or short phrases quickly.

Useful Features of the Mobile App

It's worth getting the free mobile app if you like to use Translate while traveling. One especially useful feature is the ability to download particular languages for use offline. To do this, go to Settings, then Offline Translation. Tap the "plus" icon to get into the list of languages. These language sets are quite small in terms of file size—between 35 and 45 Mb each—so they won't take up much room on your phone. Select your language and it will download to your phone for using when you're offline.

One of my favorite features of the app is the live visual translations. With this, you can point your phone at a sign or any printed text and see a live translation overlaid on top of the image (without even snapping a photo). This is possible because Google acquired

the company that made the augmented reality app called Word Lens and integrated its technology. To use this feature, open the Translate app and tap the camera icon. It uses the language choices you previously used, so make sure that it's set to the choice you want before using the camera.

I found this handy when I wanted to understand food labels in Budapest. I pointed it at a bottle of fresh fruit juice from a juice bar and learned that the ingredients were apple, lemon, and extra ginger.

Google reminds you that the live visual translation doesn't work for all of the languages yet, only about 30 of them.

One last feature that's good to know about is Conversation Mode. Normally the app listens for one language at a time, but with this feature, you can have it listen for two languages at once. This is handy for talking with someone, handing the phone back and forth and speaking into it. You'll each see the translation of what the other said. Use the button in the middle of the app to switch to this mode. During the World Cup events in 2018, several news stories came out about fans using Google Translate to communicate. During the event, Google reported a 30 percent increase in sessions from Russia using mobile phones, with the highest number of translations between Spanish and Russian, and Arabic and Russian.[1]

Google Books

Google Books is a great place to find free, public domain e-books to download. It's also good for reading previews of books still under copyright since many publishers make book previews available there.

It's especially useful for searching the full text of books. When you search Google Books, you're searching Google's database of books instead of websites crawled by Google. This database contains scanned public domain e-books and publisher previews of books still under copyright. The scanned books are from their Library Project, https://books.google.com/intl/en/googlebooks/library, and the publisher previews are from the Partner Program, https://books.google.com/intl/en/googlebooks/partners. (It's worth reading Google's help page about how those programs work to fully understand the scope of their database.) With Google Books, you're searching the full text of these books, even if you can only view certain sections of those books that publishers have made available as previews. That makes it a good place to find the source of particular quotes or writings.

To begin, go to https://books.google.com and enter the name of a public domain book, such as **Wonderful Wizard of Oz**. You can also begin on the main Google search page and then switch to the Books tab on your results screen. After you do this, click the Tools menu and look for some useful filters to appear. The date filter is especially useful—find it under the "Any Time" menu.

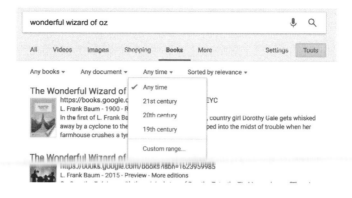

Under each result, after the author and date, you'll see one of these options as a link: No preview, Preview, or Read. Look for a Read link to see an edition that's in the public domain and free to read. Click on "Read" or click on the title to enter the reading interface.

You can read the book in your desktop browser or in the Google Play Books mobile app. You can also download a copy to read in any e-reading app or device—usually, both PDF and EPUB formats are available. In your desktop browser, look for the gear icon to find the Settings menu. In that menu, you can switch between plain text and page images. (Many of these books have been scanned from library copies.) The mobile app has similar choices for switching views.

Google also provides links for buying books from various booksellers, and for borrowing books from libraries, using WorldCat to connect to your local libraries.

Searching Inside of Books

Let's say you want to find out the source of this quote: "the really efficient laborer will not crowd his day with work." Enter it in the Books search box and you'll quickly find out that it was Henry David Thoreau. Click into the Preview of *The Heart of Thoreau's Journals*, and you'll be brought directly to the page that contains that sentence. It's useful to see the context of the quote by reading the surrounding text.

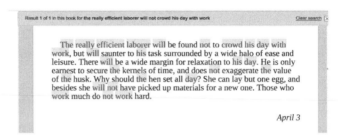

Another useful feature is the About This Book page. Find the link to it in the left sidebar under the box called "search in this book." This page brings together many useful bits of information, including reviews, related books, the table of contents, links to other editions, a tag cloud of common words and phrases from the book (click a tag to find page previews in the book that contain it), about the author, and a full bibliographic citation with links for exporting it to EndNote and other citation managers.

Common terms and phrases

advertising Agriculture aid's American Burger King California Carl Carl Karcher Carl's Carl's Jr cattle chemicals chicken Cited coli Colorado Springs ConAgra consumers contaminated customers decade Donald's Drive-In earn economic employees executives farmers fast food chains fast food industry fast food restaurants fast food workers Teamster federal feedlots flavor food safety foodborne franchise french fries frozen Greeley ground beef hamburger Ibid IBP's Idaho injuries Interview J. R. Simplot Journal Kenny kids kitchen labor land large meatpacking largest Little Caesars manager McDon McDonald's Corporation McLibel meat meatpacking meatpacking industry million minimum wage Monfort National obesity OSHA outbreak pathogens percent Pizza plant Plauen potatoes poultry pounds processors production Quoted ranch ranchers Ray Kroc roughly selling slaughter slaughterhouse sold suppliers Taco Bell taste teenagers ton Today told town union United USDA Walt Disney Wendy's World York

Tag cloud from the book, Fast Food Nation.

If a book has been quoted by others, you'll see a section on the About page, called "popular passages."

For example, in *Fast Food Nation*, a popular passage is, "This is rat eat rat, dog eat dog. I'll kill 'em, and I'm going to kill 'em before they kill me." Follow the link below it that says, "Appears in

10 books from 1982–2004," and you'll find a list of books that contain that passage, which happens to be a quote from Ray Kroc, the founder of McDonald's. Click into any of those titles to see the pages that contain that passage.

Books 1 - 5 of 5 on **This is not. This is rat eat rat, dog eat dog. I'll kill 'em, and I'm going to kill....**

❝ This is not. This is rat eat rat, dog eat dog. I'll kill 'em, and I'm going to kill 'em before they kill me ❞

Fast Food Nation: The Dark Side of the All-American Meal - Page 37
by Eric Schlosser - 2001 - 356 pages
Limited preview - About this book

Making Fast Food: From the Frying Pan Into the Fryer

Ester Reiter - Business & Economics - 1996 - 225 pages
...market - the family. CHAPTER THREE The Fast Food Invasion It is ridiculous to call this an industry. **This is not. This is rat eat rat, dog eat dog. I'll kill 'em** before they kill me. You're talking about the American way of survival of the fittest. Ray Kroc, founder...
Limited preview - About this book

We Are What We Eat

Donna R. Gabaccia - Cooking - 2000 - 288 pages
...his own success, Kroc also insisted to an interviewer, "It is ridiculous to call this an industry. **This is not. This is rat eat rat, dog eat dog. I'll kill 'em** before they kill me. You're talking about the American way of survival of the fittest."49 That was...
Limited preview - About this book

An Era of Addiction: The Evolution of Dependency

W. L. Houser-Thomas - Self-Help - 2002 - 204 pages
...Disney's footsteps who decades later was Ray Kroc who stated his political philosophy as the following, **"Look, it is ridiculous to call this an industry,"...**"This is not. This is rat eat rat, dog eat dog. I'll kiU'em, and I'm going to kiU'em before they kill me. You're talking about the American way of survival...
Limited preview - About this book

THE   The Quotable Tycoon: An Irreverent Collection of

From Fast Food Nation, https://tinyurl.com/y9o4jxqy

Google Books also has an Advanced Search screen. Find it from the Settings menu of your results screen. This screen is self-explanatory, with useful features such as limiting to books with a full view only, limiting by date, and searching by ISBN.

The main thing to keep in mind about searching in Google Books is that with the ability to search inside of books, and with so many previews available, you can find a great deal of useful information that may not be on open web pages. And even though you may not be able to read the entire book without buying it or borrowing it, it can give you enough information to decide whether the book is worth getting.

Google Scholar

Google Scholar, https://scholar.google.com, is a very useful way to search peer-reviewed scholarly content. It indexes the following types of content:

- most peer-reviewed online academic journals and books
- conference papers
- theses and dissertations
- preprints
- abstracts
- technical reports
- court opinions
- patents

Google doesn't publish a list of journals that they index, but one study estimates that it includes 90 percent of all scholarly documents on the web (written in English).[2]

Features to Look For

On the results screen, there are several useful features. You can limit by date by using the filter links in the left sidebar. For example, I entered the terms **mobile computing in higher education**, and the first three results were from 2013, 2011, and 2004 respectively.

If you want newer articles, try the links marked "since 2017," "since 2018," or "custom range." You can also change the default relevance sort to "by date."

An especially useful feature of Scholar is the "cited by" link. You can find it under each article result, with a link such as "cited by 8." Follow that link to find other scholarly articles that have cited the source you are viewing. This is a very useful way to find other papers on the same topic.

Exploring undergraduate students' usage pattern of **mobile** apps for **education**
ISH Wai, SSY Ng, DKW Chiu... - ... of Librarianship and ..., 2018 - journals.sagepub.com
In recent years, with the general adoption of smartphones with computing power comparable
to desktop computers, mobile applications (apps) have experienced a su...
☆ 〃 Cited by 8 Related articles All 2 versions

You can also use the "related articles" link to find more articles that are related in some way other than citing the source.

Getting the Articles

Since many scholarly articles are behind paywalls, it's useful to tell Google Scholar which libraries you have access to. This works for libraries that have set up their system to work with Google Scholar—this includes academic and many larger public and special libraries. If you don't set this up, you'll usually find only an abstract, with links to purchase the article from its publisher, and those are usually quite expensive.

To choose your libraries, go to Settings, look for the menu that pops out on the left when clicking the three lines, and look for the Gear icon at the top.

On the settings screen, look for the link called "library links." Here you can enter up to five libraries that you have access to. Libraries will show up if they have set up access to Google Scholar. For example, I have access to the Boston Public Library and Central European University Library, so I've entered those in my settings.

Once you've added your libraries, links will show in the results that lead you to sources that are part of that library's subscriptions.

Look on the right side of the screen for those links. Most libraries have links that look like these examples: findit@CEULibrary or Full-Text@BPL. Those links will bring you to that library's version through whatever steps you usually do to authenticate yourself to that library.

Getting Free Copies

Google Scholar is helpful for finding free copies of scholarly articles too. Many articles in subscription journals also have a free version somewhere on the open web, such as from the author's own website or an open access repository. Google helpfully indicates these in the same sidebar—look for links that are usually PDFs, such as **[PDF] ed.gov**.

To learn more about Google Scholar, read the help pages from Google, found at https://scholar.google.com/intl/en/scholar/help .html.

Google Maps

Google Maps is one of those tools that many people use frequently for getting directions—so you're probably familiar with the basics. However, there are some lesser-known features that are worth understanding. I'll discuss three of those: the "time travel" feature, viewing the inside of certain buildings, and viewing floor plans.

Google Street View: Time Travel

If you want to find out what a particular place looked like a few years ago (or anytime since Google Maps began photographing it in 2007), you can use the time travel feature. This feature shows you previous versions of Google Street View photos on a timeline going back to the first photograph that Google took of it. Of course this only works for places that Google has photographed for Street View.

To do this, use a desktop browser and go to https://www .google.com/maps. (This is not available in the mobile app.) Locate the place you are interested in, perhaps the site where a new building was constructed recently. Enter "Street View" in the usual way, by dragging the small yellow man icon to the street or intersection that you want to view. This will bring up Google's latest 360-degree photos of that location. The month and year of that photo appears at the bottom of the page, for example, "Image capture: Jan 2017."

Look for a small square overlay in the upper left of the photo, where you'll see a clock icon and the month/year of the current photo, representing "time travel." Click on that to see the oldest photo that Google has of that location. Drag the large dot along the timeline from the oldest date back to the newest one, and along the way you'll see each photo that Google has for that location.

If you want to try an example, search for 84 S. 5th Ave., Tucson, Arizona. This is a site where a new hotel was constructed in 2017 and 2018. As of this writing in June of 2018, the newest photo is from January of 2017, showing the building under construction. (The building is now finished, something I know since I live near that location.) Google may have a newer photo of the finished hotel by the time you read this.

Street view timeline dragged to the left for the earliest photo from January 2008.

You can see in the photo that there is a colorful mural across the street from the construction site. If you go back in time you'll see an empty space before the mural was painted, and you'll see an empty lot where the building was constructed.

Street view timeline in the middle view, showing a photo from July 2013.

Here are some ideas for how this can be useful:

- See new buildings at different stages of construction.
- View examples of street art (such as murals) that have been removed from a location.
- See damage to a location before and after a natural disaster.

Google captures images by car, by the Street View Trekker (used on a backpack in remote locations), by the Street View Trolley (for taking photos inside of museums and other buildings), by snowmobile, and by the Street View Trike. You can see pictures of Google's fleet at their page called "Where We've Been & Where We're Headed Next," https://www.google.com/streetview/ understand. On that page you can select a country from the menu to see a list of cities, towns, and regions where they are currently and soon to be photographing. Anyone can contribute photos to Google Maps, and if they are accepted, the photographer will be credited.

See Inside Buildings

Another interesting feature of Google Maps is the ability to see inside certain buildings. Google has mapped many museums, airports, malls, stadiums, and transit centers with indoor photos.[3]

One of my favorite places to view inside is the Museum of Antique Toys in Mexico City (Museo del Juguete Antiguo México), https://goo.gl/maps/ZYZzrvCmEVS2. I visited the museum in 2015 and not only is it filled with old toys, but the walls (inside and out) are full of amazing murals and street art. (Read the story of how I found the museum in my blog post, https://locationflexiblelife.com/2013/10/02/a-unique-place -to-see-street-art-in-mexico-city/.) When you drag the little yellow

man icon to a place with interior views, you'll see blue lines throughout, showing the path the photographers took. Drop the icon on one of those lines and you'll see the interior view at that spot. You can navigate through the building by clicking on arrows on the floor, in the same way as you navigate through streets.

Another place to view beautiful interiors is the Nasir al-Mulk Mosque, in Shiraz, Iran, https://goo.gl/maps/yzMRLd7juo42. Be sure to look up at the beautiful designs on the ceiling. Google features some interesting interior views on their pages about how Street View works. See views from the tallest building in the world, Burj Khalifa, on this page, https://www .google.com/maps/about/behind-the-scenes/streetview/treks/ burj-khalifa/. Learn more about interior navigation from Google here, https://www.google.com/maps/about/partners/ indoormaps/.

View Floor Plans

You can also view floor plans of many airports, malls, stadiums, and transit centers. This works on both desktop browsers and the Google Maps mobile app for iOS and Android. See https:// www.google.com/maps/about/partners/indoormaps/. To see an example, look up San Francisco International Airport in Google Maps, https://goo.gl/maps/TyDyyZ56SQP2. Zoom in to one of the terminals until you see "1, 2, 3" above the zoom

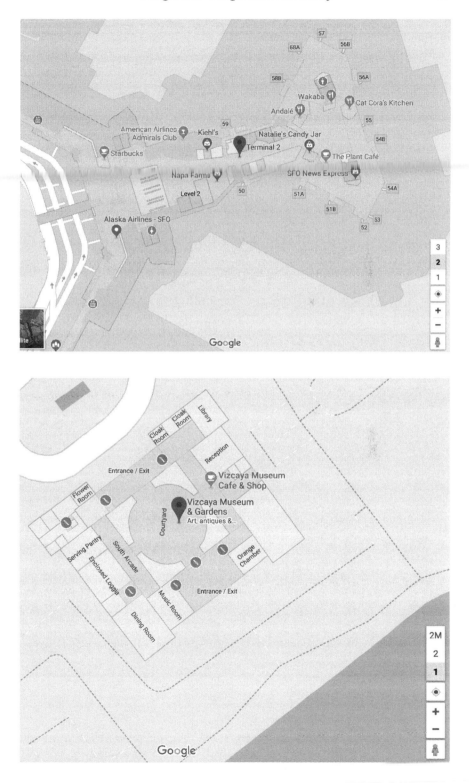

controls. These are the floor numbers and you can click on one of them to see a floor plan for that level. Everything worth seeing is on level 2 for that location. For another example, see the Vizcaya Museum & Gardens in Miami, Florida, https://goo.gl/maps/o1guyBMacZT2. Click on 1, 2, or 2M to see the levels of the museum. You can also drag the Street View icon to a room on one of those floors to see interior 360-degree photos.

Learn more about indoor locations on Google Maps in their FAQ, https://maps.google.com/help/maps/indoormaps/faqs.html. A few years ago Google provided a complete list of locations with indoor maps on this page, https://support.google.com/maps/answer/1685827?hl=en&topic=1685871. But now that they have over 10,000 locations mapped, they only list the countries that have indoor maps. So you may want to check this list first to make sure the map you're looking for is in a country that has been mapped. Even if it is, only selected locations have been mapped, usually larger and more well-known places.

Chapter 3

Multimedia Searching

Google Images Search

There are several useful tools online for finding images, including images that are licensed for reuse or free to use. Use these when you need an image for a blog post, a social media post, or printed posters and flyers.

Filtering by Color

A good place to start is Google Images, https://images.google .com. I'd like to use an example with the age-old, stereotypical question that librarians sometimes get. Your patron is trying to remember the name of a book he saw at a bookstore. He doesn't remember the title or the author, but he knows that it's on the *New York Times* best seller list and it has a yellow cover. With Google Images, you have a chance at finding it.

Go to images.google.com and enter **new york times best sellers**. Look for the Tools menu on the results screen. When you select it, several submenus will appear, including one for filtering by color. Choose yellow and you'll see images that include many book covers that are yellow. Scroll through this very long list and you might help the patron recognize the book. You'll find a few other images from pages that mention your phrase, but in this case, most of these happen to be book covers.

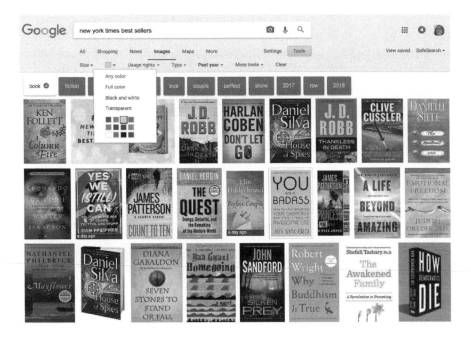

Other Useful Filters

Several other useful filters appear when you choose Tools on a Google Images results screen. In addition to color, there is time, type, usage rights, and "more tools."

Let's say you are looking for a picture of students studying, for a blog post or Facebook post you're going to write for your library. You could start by entering **students studying** at images.google.com. Let's say you've decided that images with white backgrounds will look best. You can set the color filter to white to find images that are mostly white. Next look at the "type" menu where you see the following choices: face, photo, clip art, line drawing, and animated. For your purpose, you could select photo.

The size menu is helpful if you want to narrow to particular sizes. Choices include large, medium, icon, larger than (with submenu of choices), and exactly. With the exactly choice you can enter exact values for width and height. If you'd rather not filter by size, you might find the More Tools option helpful because it includes "show sizes." This will indicate the size of each image on your results in a small overlay. For our example (looking for an image to use in a blog post), let's not bother with sizes, since for digital use you can always crop an image to the size needed. Size filtering would be useful if you are looking for large, high-resolution photos for printing.

Usage Rights Filter

Next, visit the usage rights menu and select "labeled for reuse." There are several other choices in that menu that refer to different types of Creative Commons licenses. I'll discuss these choices in the next section. For now, you want to make sure your image has the type of license that will allow you to reuse it on your site.

When you find an image you might want to use, click on it, and you'll see choices that include "web." Follow that link to find the source of the image so you can further investigate whether or not it has a license that allows for reuse.

In the example shown here, there is an "i" button on the photo. (Find the image here, https://www.jisc.ac.uk/blog/students-experiences -and-expectations-of-the-digital-environment-23-jun-2014.) Clicking it opens an overlay with a link marked "CCBY." If you are familiar with Creative Commons licensing, you'll recognize that acronym as their "CC BY 3.0" license. Follow the link to learn that you can use it as long as you give credit to the author.[1] The page from Creative Commons says that you can share it in any format and adapt it for any purpose, even commercially.

In the next section, I'll discuss other tools for finding images with licenses that allow for reuse, along with more information about Creative Commons licensing.

Finding Images with Licenses That Allow Reuse

Creative Commons licenses are designed to give creators ways to grant permissions to reuse their work. They offer different levels of copyright licenses that allow you to find a balance between offering your work as "all rights reserved" and making it completely free to use. There are six different levels of licenses, and you can read the details of each one at https://creativecommons.org/licenses.

If you would like to assign one of these licenses to your own creative work, visit https://creativecommons.org/choose. Here you can decide whether you want adaptations of your work to be shared, whether you want to allow commercial use of your work, and a few other options. After you make your selections, the appropriate license is displayed. There is also an icon and some code you can add to your own web pages that will link back to this site.

Creative Commons offers a search tool for finding images with these licenses across several open archives at https://ccsearch.creativecommons.org. Enter some keywords and choose which license features you want (such as being able to modify, adapt, or build upon).

Other Search Tools for Reusable Images

There are several other good tools for finding images to reuse. Here are some of the best ones.

Flickr Advanced Search   https://www.flickr.com/search/advanced

If you aren't finding what you need with Google Images search, Flickr is a good place to search next. Its huge archive of photos has

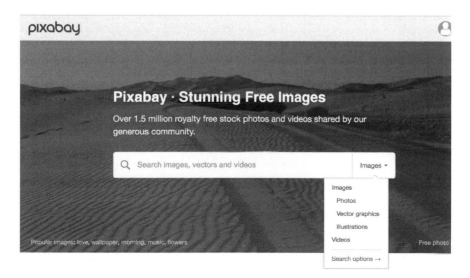

many images with Creative Commons licenses. Use their Advanced Search screen and look for the menu marked "Any license." Choices there include the following: All creative commons, Commercial use allowed, Modifications allowed, Commercial use & mods allowed, No known copyright restrictions, and U.S. Government works. Flickr also offers filters for color, size, date taken, and your choice of photos or videos. You can browse Creative Commons photos on Flickr at https://www.flickr.com/creativecommons.

Pixabay   https://pixabay.com

Another great tool for finding images that are free to use is Pixabay. What makes this site unique is that all of their images are copyright-free (Creative Commons CC0), so you can use them even for commercial purposes, without asking for permission or giving credit.

You can enter keywords and filter by photos, vector graphics, illustrations, or videos. If you create a free account, you can mark images as favorites. This is a handy place to keep a list of images you might want to use someday in blog posts, social media posts, print flyers, or presentations. If you want to use advanced search features, see their instructions at https://pixabay.com/en/blog/posts/advanced-image-search-on-pixabay-46. Be sure to look for the filters found on every results page. With these, you can filter your search by color, size, orientation, and more.

Unsplash   https://unsplash.com

One more useful tool for finding free images is Unsplash. All of their photos can be used for free, even for commercial purposes, and even for adapting or modifying. You don't need to ask for permission or give credit to the photographer, though it is a nice gesture to do so.[2]

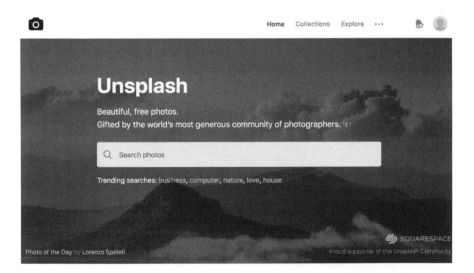

Unsplash's collections are particularly strong in beautiful photos of landscapes, architecture, and astronomy. You can find many other types of images there as well. You can search by entering keywords on their home page, or you can browse collections that others have made at https://unsplash.com/collections. These large, beautiful photos often work well for desktop backgrounds on your computers or mobile devices. If you make a free account, you can save your "liked" photos, and also make your own collections of photos you find there.

When you are on the results screen for a search, look for the terms across the top, under the search box. These are keywords that appear in the photos you've found, and you can click on them to narrow your search. For example, after search spiral staircase, you find terms such as stairwell, architecture, library, and more.

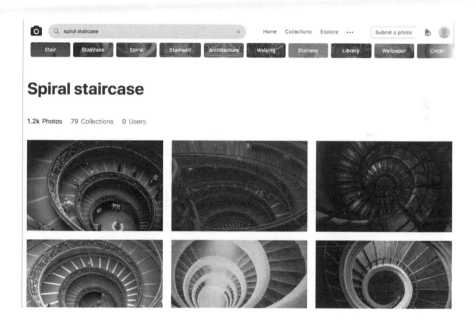

Unsplash also has a mobile app for iOS.[3] This makes it easy to find photos for use in creative projects directly on your iPhone or iPad. If you use the Chrome browser on your computer, you might enjoy the Chrome extension, called Unsplash Instant. Find it at https://instant.unsplash.com. With this installed, each new tab that you open contains a random image from Unsplash as its background. If you like a particular photo, there is an easy way to save it, with a download button superimposed on the photo.

Reverse Image Search

Another useful tool from Google Images is their reverse image search. Start at https://images.google.com and click the camera icon to "search by image."

Discover architecture through Monet's brushstrokes

This brings you to a screen where you can either search by URL (of an image online) or upload an image from your computer. This is a way to search for similar images, sites that contain the image, and different sizes of the same image that might be available.

Photo by Nicole Hennig

Let's say you have an image on your own computer—a photo of a snake you saw crossing a bike path. Upload this image and Google will find similar images, which can help you identify the snake.

On the results screen you will see, "best guess for this image: common king snake." Follow that link in the Google Images tab and you'll see many photos of this type of snake.

To further narrow the results, you'll see colorful boxes with terms from the

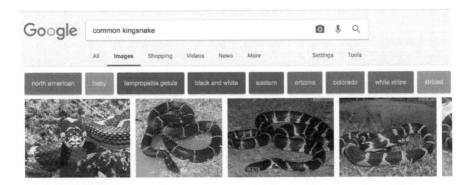

results to help you narrow it down. In my case, some of the words were: North American, baby, Lampropeltis Getula, Arizona, and Colorado.

This example image is of a snake I photographed on a bike trail. After my reverse image search, I still wasn't sure if Google was showing me images of the same type of snake, so I clicked on the filter for **Arizona**, since I took the photo on a bike path in Tucson. From this set of results, I could see that some of these snakes are red, like the one I had photographed, and that they are found in Arizona.

You can also use the Tools menu on the results screen to bring up more filters, such as the one for color. I chose red from that menu and found many images that looked very similar to my original photo. By following some of the links that contained those photos, I found out that it was likely a common king snake. These snakes are found in my area, and I learned that they aren't poisonous.

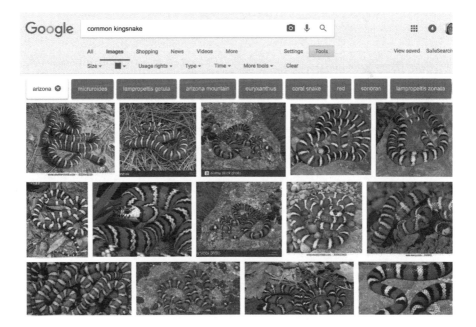

This type of reverse image search can be useful for other kinds of identification, such as plants, insects, architectural styles, products, or objects that you don't know the name of.

There are other ways to use this type of search as well. Here are a few examples.

- You can usually find the artist of a particular computer desktop wallpaper that doesn't tell you the source.
- If you see a piece of artwork in a public place, you can photograph it and use reverse image search to find out who the artist is and where you can buy it or a similar artwork.
- Some people use it to identify a celebrity by taking a photo of a person on their television screen. Reverse image searches can often find similar images and tell you who the person is.
- If you want to find out whether a social media profile is a fake one, you can use reverse image search to upload the photo. Often fake profiles use common stock photography, and if it's fake, it's likely to show up on a stock photography website.
- In a similar way, you can use it to debunk viral posts or memes that claim to be a current photo but are actually from several years ago in another situation.
- If you are a photographer or artist, you could use a reverse image search to see if your own work is appearing on other websites (with or without your permission).

Learn more on Google's help pages, https://support.google.com/websearch/answer/1325808?hl=en.

Searching for Videos on Google

When you are looking for videos, it's useful to begin with Google. That's because Google indexes video content from many different sites, not just YouTube (which they own).

Let's say you are looking for videos of lectures that happened at Howard University. On the main Google search screen, you could enter **howard university lectures**. Since much of this content is from videos, Google will show "videos" as one of the options on the results screen. Click on that to filter your results to only videos.

Remember that the Tools menu will bring up more submenus for further filtering on any Google results page. When you are on video results, the submenus are for filtering by duration, time, quality, closed captioned videos, and source.

If you are looking for recent videos, you could select "past year" in the time menu. You could also look for longer lectures in the duration menu. The choices there are short (0–4 minutes), medium (4–20 minutes), and long (20+ minutes).

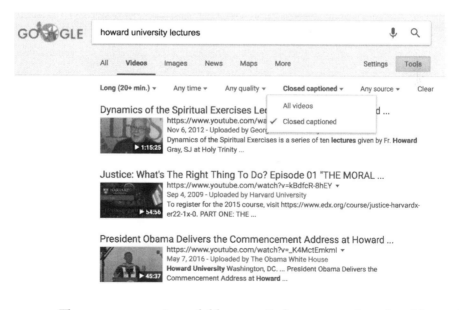

Another useful filter helps you find closed-captioned videos. Look in the menu marked "all videos" to see the closed captioned filter option.

The source menu is useful because it shows you where the videos in your results set can be found. YouTube is so large that it's usually the first choice. For my search, it's useful to know that some of these lectures can be also found on c-span.org, harvard.edu, time.com, and howard.edu.

The sources option can also help you discover video sites that contain certain types of video. For example, if you are looking for examples of stop-motion animation, you could enter **stop motion animation** on the main Google search screen, then click on Videos. Use the source filter to see which sites other than YouTube have this type of animation—sites like https://vimeo.com, https://gizmodo.com, and https://laughingsquid.com.

There is also an advanced search screen for videos at https://www.google.com/advanced_video_search. This works in the same way as the advanced Google search discussed in Chapter 1, with a few additions. On this screen you can choose to narrow your search by quality (any or HD only); subtitles (any or closed captioned only); and safe search (filter explicit results). Use this screen for those features.

YouTube Filters

When you begin your video search on YouTube, it's easy to miss one of the most useful features—filters. On the results page of a search from your computer, look on the left side, above the results for the word 'filter' with an icon that looks like three slider bars. On your mobile device in the YouTube app results screen, look for the same icon. This filtering choice will bring up several useful filters and sorting options.

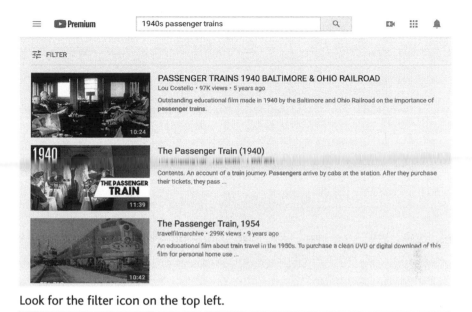

Look for the filter icon on the top left.

Follow this link to get several useful filters: upload date, type, duration, and features.

Let's say you are searching for old videos of 1940s passenger trains that you can use for free on a website. After you enter **1940s passenger trains**, use the Features filter to choose Creative Commons. You can also use the Duration filter to select short (less than 4 minutes) or long (greater than 20 minutes).

Other filter options you may find useful are found in the Feature menu: 4K, HD, HDR, Subtitles/CC, Creative Commons, 3D, Live, Purchased, 360 degrees, and Location. Use "Live" to find live streams from webcams, useful for viewing rocket launches from NASA, for example. Videos from this filtered set are recordings of live broadcasts, and if the stream is currently live, you'll see a "live now" button.

Finding Videos with Captions

Use Subtitles/CC to find videos that have captions available. Captions are always good to have for hard of hearing users or for people viewing with their sound turned off. To see the captions for a video, look for CC in a white box on the bottom right side of the video. Click on that to turn captions or subtitles on and to select your language (if multiple languages are available). If you are using the mobile app, you may have to tap lightly on the video itself to see this option. It's found under the icon that looks like

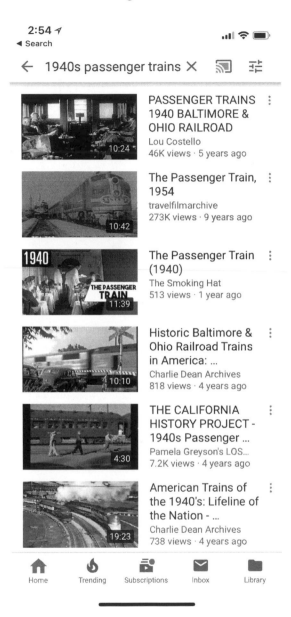

Look for 3 slider bars icon in upper right to find the filters in the mobile app.

three dots in a vertical line. Google has added auto-generated captions to most videos on YouTube in about 10 supported languages (English, Dutch, French, German, Italian, Japanese, Korean, Portuguese, Russian, and Spanish). However, these captions aren't

About 24,700 results				☰ FILTER
UPLOAD DATE	**TYPE**	**DURATION**	**FEATURES**	**SORT BY**
Last hour	Video	Short (< 4 minutes)	4K	Relevance
Today	Channel	Long (> 20 minutes)	HD	Upload date
This week	Playlist		HDR	View count
This month	Movie		Subtitles/CC	Rating
This year	Show		Creative Commons	
			3D	
			Live	
			Purchased	
			360°	
			Location	

Dr. Vandana Shiva - Author, Activist, Pioneer, Scientific Advisor, Mother - Soil Not Oil 2017 -

Look for the CC icon on the lower right to turn on captions.

---

perfect and often have errors. Anyone who uploads video to YouTube can add their own accurate captions. Instructions can be found online for how to do this.[4]

Finding Channels and Playlists

The Type menu includes video, channel, playlist, movie, or show. When you are searching a broad topic, let's say, **Native American history**, filter by channel to find content producers that are devoted to that topic. If you find one that looks good, like Smithsonian National Museum of the American Indian, https://www.youtube.com/user/SmithsonianNMAI, you can subscribe to the channel on their page, and get updates when they post new content.

Filter your broad topic by Playlist to find sets of videos that people have collected on your topic. Both Channel and Playlist are useful for finding curated collections of content, rather than browsing randomly through the many videos found under a broad search.

Vimeo Search

You might remember, from the section about Google Video filters, that you can find videos from sites other than YouTube in the source menu. One of those sites that often comes up for certain types of videos is Vimeo.com. Vimeo is a great place to search for high-quality videos made by independent creators. It's used by many professional filmmakers and video producers as a place to host and showcase their content, and it doesn't show ads. Vimeo hosts both free and paid content, and you can filter by free or paid on your results screen.

You can browse in the following categories (https://vimeo.com/categories): animation, arts & design, cameras & techniques, comedy, documentary, experimental, fashion, food, instructionals, music, narrative, personal, reporting & journalism, sports, talks, and travel. Each of those categories has useful subcategories as well. Let's say you are looking for examples of stop-motion animation. Go to the animation category and select "stop frame" as your subcategory, https://vimeo.com/categories/animation/stopmotion/videos. Using the filters on your results, you can refine by date uploaded, duration, license (including Creative Commons licenses), and more. Another way to browse is to look through Vimeo's Channels (https://vimeo.com/channels) and Groups (https://vimeo.com/groups).

You can also enter terms in Vimeo's search box and find useful filters on the results screens. Let's say you want to find free films about planets, uploaded in the last year, with a Creative Commons license. You could enter **planets** in the search box, https://vimeo.com/search?q=planets, then filter by date uploaded=last 365 days, price=free, and license=CC BY, https://vimeo.com/search?license=by&price=free&q=planets&uploaded=this-year. If you want to, you could further filter by categories, such as animation, documentary, travel, talks, and more. If you're not seeing all of the filters on the results screen, be sure to look for the "more filters" link, which will expand the choices. You can learn more about Vimeo's search features on their help page, found at https://help.vimeo.com/hc/en-us/articles/224818227-Searching-for-videos.

Vimeo is an important site to be familiar with if you want to find professionally produced videos. It's especially strong in the arts, animation, independent documentaries, and experimental film.[5]

Chapter 4

Social Media Searching

Twitter Search

Twitter may have a reputation for various kinds of bad behavior, like harassment, racism, and fake news, but it's also useful for several important kinds of information. What can you find using Twitter?

- Firsthand reports of events as they happen (such as natural disasters, protests, sporting events, or awards ceremonies)
- Conversation threads for conferences and other events
- Technical support from companies by direct message
- Links to published content, curated by people who care about particular topics
- Comments from people about a particular company, university, or other institution
- Humor, quotes, and productivity advice

You can find the search box in the top bar of Twitter's website, the bottom bar of Twitter's mobile app, or you can go to this page: https://twitter.com/search-home.

Top versus Latest

Let's try a basic keyword search of Twitter. If you enter the term **earthquake japan** in the search box, your results will default to "Top" tweets. These are tweets that are getting a lot of engagement—retweets, likes, and so forth. If you want to find the latest tweets, be sure to look for the tab called "Latest" and switch to that. Entering two keywords like that is a very broad search.

Advanced search

Words

All of these words

This exact phrase

Any of these words

None of these words

These hashtags

Written in   All languages   ♦

People

From these accounts

To these accounts

Mentioning these accounts

Places

Near this place   ⊚ Japan

Dates

From this date   _____ to _____

Search

A more useful way to find out about earthquakes that just happened in a particular area is to use the advanced search screen, https://twitter.com/search-advanced, and limit by location.

Twitter Advanced Search

One useful feature on the advanced search is the location filter, called Places. If you have location services turned on for your computer or mobile device, it will default to the location where you are connected to the internet. You can change this by clicking on the location name. This brings up a search box where you can enter the name of a neighborhood, city, or country. When looking for tweets about earthquakes in Japan that happened recently (or are happening right now), you could use the advanced screen to enter **earthquake japan** and use the Places menu to filter to a particular city or region in Japan. That will result in tweets from that location (for people who have location services turned on).

You can use this feature to find information about events in the past as well. Try searching for **thailand cave rescue**, with the Place set to Chiang Rai, Thailand, and the dates set to "**From: 2018-07-06 To: 2018-07-10**." This will find tweets from people in that location during those few days. These might provide interesting perspectives that are different from or complementary to what ends up in the news. Many news reporters from around the world were there, so it's possible to turn up tweets in English if you don't read Thai. You can also use the language filter on the advanced search to limit results to a particular language.

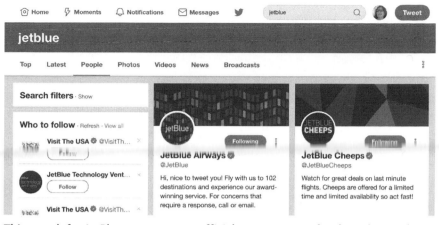

This search for JetBlue turns up two official accounts, one for the airline and one for deals from the airline (@JetBlueCheeps).

Finding Tweets from One User to Another User

Another type of search that can be useful is the "from and to" search. You can use this to find mentions of a particular user in another user's tweets. This works for both individuals and companies or other organizations. On the advanced screen in the People section, enter one person's Twitter handle in "From these accounts" and the other in "To these accounts." You will need to make sure you know the correct Twitter handle for each. To find a handle, do a quick search for the person's or company's name in the main Twitter box and switch to the People tab on your results screen.

DIRECTV and Viacom are known for sparring with each other on Twitter. To see their conversations, try **from:viacom to:directv** or the reverse. This can be a useful way to learn more about companies or organizations and how they compete or otherwise interact.

People

From these accounts	viacom
To these accounts	directv
Mentioning these accounts	

Places

Near this place   ⊙ Add location

Dates

From this date   to

Search

Filters

One feature that's easy to miss is the filter option on the Twitter results screen. On desktop web browsers it's found in the left sidebar,

privacy library data

Top   Latest   People   Photos   V

Search filters · Show

but it's hidden by default. You need to click "Show" next to Search Filters to see the actual filter choices. In the mobile app, it's found in the search box itself (after you do a search). To use it, tap on the icon that looks like two slider bars.

On the results screen of any search, no matter where you began, it's always good to look for those filters and decide if they might be useful for your results. You can filter by location, language, and by "people you follow." If you are searching for a topic that is often tweeted about by people you follow, that filter can be quite useful. I searched for **privacy library data** and found interesting results from the people I follow since I follow many librarians who tweet about that topic. This is worth trying if you're getting too many false hits in results that include everyone.

Hashtags

Searching by hashtag is one of the most useful aspects of Twitter. If you see a word with a # sign in front of it, that's a hashtag. It's used to bring together tweets on a similar topic, and it's also used to express humor, sarcasm, and other commentary. When you click or tap on it, you'll see other tweets that contain that hashtag.

Hashtags can't contain spaces or other punctuation, but they can contain numbers and use capital letters to make it easier to read words that are run together. For example, #StopTheViolence is used for tweets about gun violence. Hashtags are not case-sensitive,

so you can enter #stoptheviolence, and it will find both capitalized and non-capitalized tags.

Conferences and other events usually announce specific hashtags for particular sessions. That makes it easy to follow what people are tweeting about that event, while it happens and afterward. For example, #sxswedu is the hashtag for South by Southwest EDU, the conference that happens every March in Austin, Texas.

Be aware that some hashtags are used for more than one purpose, so you may find results that aren't what you expected. For example, #TopTechTrends has been used in the past to tweet about the event of that name that happens at American Library Association conferences. But it's also used by anyone who wants to tweet about technology trends. So for recent events, ALA announced this more unique tag: #ALATT.

If you know of a specific hashtag, you can enter it in the Twitter search box. Be sure to include the # sign. You can also use the advanced search screen and fill in your hashtag (without the #) into the field called "these hashtags." But be aware that terms entered into that field will be searched with a Boolean OR. So if you want to find tweets with multiple hashtags, use the main search box and enter your hashtags with the AND operator between them. For example, **#alaac18 and #alattt**.

To learn more about hashtags, see Twitter's help page on the topic at https://help.twitter.com/en/using-twitter/how-to-use-hashtags. A useful guide for using hashtags on various social media sites is "The Beginner's Guide to the Hashtag," by Rebecca Hiscott, on Mashable, https://mashable.com/2013/10/08/what-is-hashtag.

Remember that with all of your Twitter searches, the results will default to "Top" (tweets with a lot of engagement), and you may often want to switch your results to "Latest" in order to see the most current tweets from everyone.

Facebook as a Search Engine

Most people don't think of Facebook when it comes to searching for information. However, it can be a valuable source for certain kinds of information and offers useful filters when you use their search tool.

If you don't have a Facebook account, you can use Google to search for public information posted by Facebook users. Do this by limiting to the domain facebook.com. Enter your terms into Google, as in this example: **site:facebook.com Noam Chomsky**. If you are searching for a very common name, you will probably have more luck if you add the current city after the person's name. When you find a person, the information you will see is only what they have made public (unless you are in their friends list; then you will also see what they have made viewable by friends). Many people make their location public, their job title, some of their interests, and some of their photos and posts. Some people have privacy settings set to not allow Google or other search engines to find them at all. If you would like to hide your profile from search engines, go to Facebook's Settings, then Privacy, and look for "Do you want search engines outside of Facebook to link to your profile?"—change it from yes to no.

If you have a Facebook account, there are many more useful search features available when you are logged in. Start by entering keywords in the search box found on the top of any page. You can

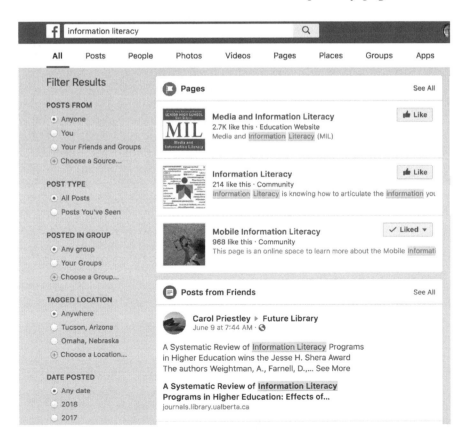

search for people, posts, videos, photos, places, groups, pages, events, and more.

A Basic Search—Finding Events, Pages, and Groups

Enter **information literacy** in the search box. Scroll down on the results screen to see Pages, Posts from Friends, Links, Public Posts, and Groups. Look across the top for links that filter your results to only Posts, People, Photos, Video, Pages, Places, Groups, Apps, Events, or Marketplace. If you choose Events, you'll see any event posted publicly, not just from those you follow or your own region. This is also a good way to find Pages or Groups about a particular topic.

Using the Filters

There are many useful filters in the left sidebar. Let's say you've searched for the word **books** and filtered to Events. Look in the sidebar for a location filter, and select your city or region. This will turn up author readings, book clubs, and discussion groups. You can also filter by "popular with friends." Facebook is a very useful way to find events related to any interest. There is also a mobile app called Facebook Local that you can use to find events in your area.

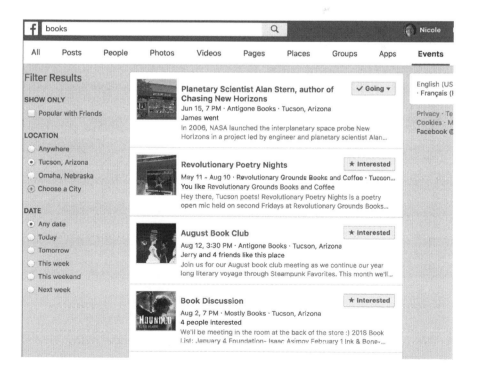

It's available for Android and iOS; see https://www.facebook
.com/local. This app is a good way to find events without getting
distracted by your entire Facebook newsfeed. It has a simple,
usable interface and gets many positive reviews.[1]

Facebook is also good for finding articles and videos from news
sources on just about any topic. Enter **water on mars** in the search
box and on the results screen select Videos from the bar at the top.
You'll see results from sources like NASA, National Geographic
TV, and other news outlets. Facebook has such huge reach that
it's rare to find publications that don't post on Facebook.[2] As with
any search, use your discrimination when selecting results, since
you'll also find results from Alltime Conspiracies (though that
could be helpful if you're researching conspiracies).

Going back to All for the **water on mars** search, try using the filters
in the left sidebar. Under "Posts From," you can select Anyone,
You, Your Friends and Groups, or you can enter a source in the
Source box. Enter Scientific American and that will filter your
results to content from them. This helps filter out false hits, such
as content from the band known as Water on Mars.

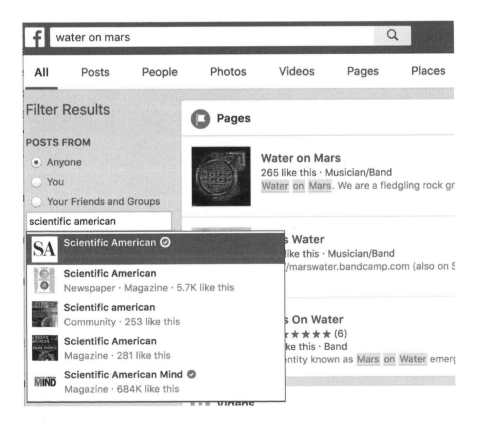

Some other useful filters in the sidebar are Date Posted, Tagged Location, and Posted in Group. It's always worth looking for filters like these in any search tool. Often they aren't obvious and you need to look around to find them.

If you are using the Facebook mobile app, you can do the same type of searching from the search box. Select from the same tabs on top of your results, such as Posts, People, and so on. After you select one of those, you'll see the filtering options. Look for Filters at the top, with an icon that looks like two slider bars.

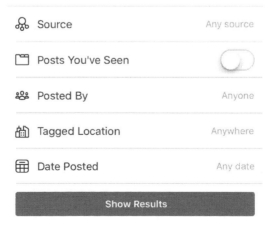

Searching by Hashtag

Like Twitter, Facebook users sometimes use hashtags to make their content more findable. For example, the hashtag #infolit is used by many people to tag content about information literacy. Enter that tag in the search box and find public posts, posts from your friends, pages, and other content about information literacy.

Searching for Photos

The Facebook photo search is handy for finding photos of yourself and your friends from any date. In the search bar enter something like one of these examples: **photos of me from 2010, photos of my friends from March, photos of [name of one of your friends]**, etc.

You can also find photos of events or topics, such as **photos of the 2017 solar eclipse**. All the same filters I've mentioned previously, apply to these searches.

Searching Your Activity Log on Facebook

If you've ever wanted to find an old post of your own from a previous year, you can use the activity search. Go to this URL: https://www.facebook.com/me/allactivity (while you are logged into Facebook) and it will show your activity log. This is a record of everything you've posted and interacted with on Facebook. You can enter terms in the box marked Activity Search and find posts that contain any keyword. For example, I entered **Budapest** in the box and found posts from my 2017 and 2015 visits to Budapest, Hungary.

Another useful feature is the list of years on the right side of your activity log. Click a particular year to see all of your activity from that year. It's interesting to see the very first post you ever made on Facebook—mine is from 2007.

In addition to searching your activity log, you can use the filters in the left sidebar. These don't work together with the activity search—they are a separate feature. You can select any of the following: Timeline Review, Photo Review, Posts, Posts You're Tagged In, Others' Posts to Your Timeline, Hidden from Timeline, Photos and Videos, Likes and Reactions, Comments.

If you select Photos and Videos, or Photos You're Tagged In, more filters will appear at the top of the screen. In the filter marked "Shared with" you can choose from See All (the default), Public,

Friends of Friends, or Friends. This makes it easy to go back and change your privacy settings on particular photos.

Finding People in Your Network with Particular Interests or Expertise

Facebook is good for finding people in your network who have particular interests or expertise. To do this, enter a term in the search box (such as libraries, or vegetarian, or Bitcoin), and on the results screen filter by "Posts From: Your Friends and Groups." This will show you everyone in your network that has posted about that topic or used that word.

According to Robert Berkman, author of *Find It Fast: Extracting Expert Information from Social Networks, Big Data, Tweets, and More*, Facebook is valuable for researchers in the following areas:

- Bottom-up, experiential, and anecdotal observations and reports, particularly from activists and passionate advocates for a cause or issue
- Insights into emerging trends via insider group members' conversations, not reported in the wider media or elsewhere online
- Strong statements of particular viewpoints on contentious public issues, especially in Facebook groups
- Clues for finding and reaching hard-to-locate people
- Possible job search leads[3]

Since Facebook is the most popular social network worldwide, with 2.2 billion monthly active users worldwide as of April 2018,[4] it's an important source of this type of information and can be part of a useful research strategy.

For more information about Facebook's search features, including how to control what others see about you, see Facebook's help page: Search Basics, https://www.facebook.com/help/460711197281324/.

Instagram Search

Instagram is useful not only for finding photos and videos of fun things posted by your friends, but also for finding information from organizations who share their news visually. The following organizations are just a few examples of this.

- National Geographic, https://www.instagram.com/natgeo
- NOAA Fisheries, https://www.instagram.com/noaafisheries
- Mars Curiosity Rover, https://www.instagram.com/marscuriosity
- Charity: water, https://www.instagram.com/charitywater
- UNICEF USA, https://www.instagram.com/unicefusa
- New York Public Library, https://www.instagram.com/nypl
- British Library, https://www.instagram.com/britishlibrary

Many organizations use Instagram to share their research, and are encouraged to do so by articles like these:

- Betty Paton, "How to Use Instagram for Research Communication," Research to Action, October 22, 2013, http://www.researchtoaction.org/2013/10/using-instagram -for-research-communication
- Paige Brown Jarreau, "Why We Scientists Do Instagram," From the Lab Bench, March 26, 2018, http://www .fromthelabbench.com/from-the-lab-bench-science-blog/2018/ 3/25/why-we-scientists-do-instagram

They do it to communicate academic research to lay audiences and to foster public interest in their work.[5]

You can search Instagram in the mobile app by tapping the search icon in the bottom bar, then tapping in the search field at the top. From there you can search everything, or just people, tags, or places.

You can also search it from your computer's web browser at https://www.instagram.com. Look for the search bar at the top of any page. If you don't have an Instagram account, you'll see a page asking you to create one, but if you don't want to have an account, you can bypass that page by following the link to any particular Instagram account, such as https://www.instagram .com/nypl. There you will see the search box at the top of the page. You can search all of Instagram that way, you just won't be able to like or comment on photos unless you have an account.

Searching by Hashtag

Hashtags are very popular on Instagram. People use them to make their photos findable in various ways. Instagram's hashtags are often keywords describing aspects of the photo, such as #bluesky, https:// www.instagram.com/explore/tags/bluesky/. Instagram is not the best tool for finding photos that are free to use on your own social media. That's because there isn't an easy way to search for images with licenses that allow reuse. Each individual photographer owns the copyright to his or her Instagram photos, so you would need to contact the photographer to ask for permission to reuse one. Instead, use the tools I mentioned in Chapter 3 for that purpose.

Here are some interesting ways to use hashtags in your search. Try looking for images of illuminated manuscripts with the hashtag #illuminatedmanuscript, https://www.instagram.com/explore/ tags/illuminatedmanuscript/. Be sure to check the plural version as well: #illuminatedmanuscripts. Here you will find photos like this one, https://www.instagram.com/p/BgzVn7_BiFH/?utm_

source=ig_web_copy_link, a manuscript of a sixteenth-century book of hours from Northern Europe, from the Cooper Hewitt Library in New York. This was posted by a library technician at Smithsonian Libraries Special Collections who goes by the Instagram name of book_historia.

If you are using the mobile app, use the Tags section of the search. You can often guess a tag by typing in the first few letters. As you type, Instagram will show a list of hashtags that exist in descending order of popularity, with the number of posts under each tag. You

3:33

Q #illuminatedmanu   Cancel

Top   People   **Tags**   Places

#illuminatedmanuscript
10.6k posts

#illuminatedmanuscripts
1682 posts

#illuminatedmanuscriptz
34 posts

#illuminatedmanusscript
26 posts

#illuminatedmanuscriptcatsofinstagram
31 posts

#illuminatedmanuscriptsofinstagram
9 posts

#illuminatedmanuscriptseries
9 posts

#illuminatedmanuacript
4 posts

#illuminatedmanucript
5 posts

#illuminatedmanuscipt
4 posts

can then select the tag of interest and possibly find other tags that will be useful.

If you are using a browser on your computer, use the top search bar on any Instagram page and enter the # sign before your word. That's how Instagram knows you want to search for a hashtag.

There are times that you may want to search for multiple hashtags at once. You can't do this within the Instagram app or web-based search pages; instead, try a Google advanced search. For example, you could enter **#illuminatedmanuscript #stars site:instagram.com** to find photos of manuscripts with images of stars. Or you could search for images of street art from Oaxaca, Mexico, with this Google search, **#oaxaca #streetart site:instagram.com**.

Another search tool for Instagram is called Mulpix, https://mulpix .com/. Their search engine accepts multiple hashtags. Try entering **oaxaca streetart**. You don't need to include the # symbol. Or try entering **satellite images**. Browsing through these results can help you find people or organizations to follow on Instagram for the types of images you are interested in seeing.

Neither Google nor Mulpix seems to have complete indexing of Instagram, so your results will vary. Use them when you want to search for multiple hashtags at once; otherwise, searching on Instagram itself will give the best results.

One more site that's worth exploring is Display-Purposes, https://display purposes.com. This search tool helps you find related hashtags to a particular one. For example, enter **#budapest** in the search box to find these related tags: #budapest, #hungary, #thisisbudapest, #moment sinbudapest, #welovebuda pest, #budapestagram,

```
#streetart                        ◉
#streetart
#graffiti
#urbanart
#streetarteverywhere
#graffitiart
#mural
#instagraffiti
#graffitiporn
#sprayart
#streetartistry
#graff
#wallart
#spraypaint
#urbanwalls
#instagraff
#wall
#stencil
#tv_streetart
#streetartphotography
#streetartist
#rsa_graffiti
#graffitiigers
#wallporn
#stencilart
#instagrafite
#stickerart
#dsb_graff
#pasteup
#instaart
#arteurbano
```

Hashtag search on displaypurposes.com.

#budapest_hungary, #insta_budapest, #ikozosseg, #danube, #buda, #loves_hungary, #magyarország, #vscohungary, #instahun, #magyarig, #ig_hun, #pest, #chainbridge, and more.

This can give you ideas for hashtags to use in your searches. Some tags have a list of frequency of their use—to see an example, search for #streetart.

Other tags don't show up at all in this engine, such as #illuminated-manuscript. It seems to be hit or miss, and they don't provide information on the scope of their tool. So your results will vary, but when it works, it's very useful.

Another potentially useful feature of this site is the Map search. Look for the Map link on the top of the screen. On this screen, you can zoom in on a map of the world to a particular location to see what hashtags are often used there. This is because many people add location tags to their Instagram photos, using the location-awareness of their mobile phone. When I zoomed in to the area near Monterey, California, I found hashtags like these, #monterey, #montereybay, #pebblebeach, #carmel, #carmelbythesea, and more.

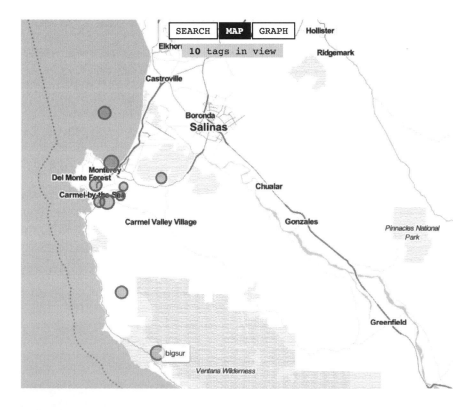

This can help you find hashtags to use when you are looking for information from a particular location. It doesn't work for every location, but when it does work, it's quite useful.

Keep in mind that Instagram and these other tools all use their own algorithms to decide what the results should be. Instagram reminds you that when you search it, the "results you see are based on a variety of factors, including the people you follow, who you're connected to and what photos and videos you like on Instagram."[6] So you will likely get different results if you are logged into your Instagram account than you would if you weren't. Keeping that in mind, don't expect precision or perfection with these searches. In spite of that, you can still find many useful photos and publications by searching Instagram.

Pinterest Search

Like Instagram, Pinterest can be used to search for more than just recipes, crafts, and fashion. Many libraries, archives, museums, publishers, scientists, researchers, and others use Pinterest to promote their work.[7] Searching Pinterest is especially useful when your topic is visual, such as art, architecture, or photography. This is because visually browsing results is much quicker than clicking on text links to see your results, as you would do with a Google search.

Pinterest is best searched when you have an account with them. A free account is all that's necessary to use all the features. You can sign up at http://pinterest.com. There is a workaround for limited searching without a Pinterest account. Visit this link, http:// pinterest.com/all, and you will bypass the signup screen and find a screen with a search bar at the top. You can begin searching there, but after clicking on a few results, Pinterest will bring you to a signup screen again. There is an option on the signup screen to "continue without account," or "browse with limited access." In my opinion, it's worth getting a free Pinterest account because then you can browse and search freely and save images into boards of your own, making them public or private.

Many book publishers use Pinterest to promote their titles. One example is the LSE Review of Books (London School of Economics), https://www.pinterest.com/lsereview/. You can choose to follow everything from a particular person or organization by clicking the red Follow button. Or you can choose to follow only particular

Access our best ideas
with a free account

Sign up to see more

> Email

> Create a password

> **Continue**

OR

> f   Continue with Facebook

> G   **Continue with Google**

By continuing, you agree to Pinterest's **Terms of Service**, **Privacy Policy**

Already a member? **Log in**

Are you a business? **Get started here**

> **Browse with limited access**

boards (topical groupings) from them. LSE Review of Books has boards on specific topics like Education, Gender Studies, Film Studies, and many more. Individual images (known as "pins") from LSE Review of Books are usually the cover of a book they have reviewed. It's nice to be able to browse by category and book cover. Each pinned cover contains a link to the book review on their website, for example, http://blogs.lse.ac.uk/lsereviewofbooks/ 2016/08/16/book-review-becoming-jane-jacobs-by-peter-l-laurence/.

A useful type of visual information that can be easily found on Pinterest is infographics. These are usually long, vertical charts that are designed to quickly and easily explain a concept or share statistics. There are infographics on many topics, for example, "The History of Augmented Reality," https://www.pinterest.com/pin/ 35606653289470138/, or "The Basics of Open Access Publishing," https://www.pinterest.com/pin/35606653287621255/. You can see my collection of infographics on various topics here, https://www .pinterest.com/nic221/infographics/.

To search, use the search bar on the top of any Pinterest screen. It's in the same place in the mobile app and on your computer's web browser. Enter a term, such as **infographics**. After you hit enter, you'll see a drop-down menu, with "All pins" as the default. With this menu, you can filter your search to Your pins, Product pins, People, or Boards.

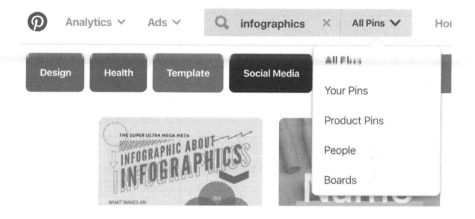

Using a system called "guided search," Pinterest suggests further keywords as you enter each term. These are shown in rectangles of different colors, just below the search bar. Let's say you've entered the term **art nouveau**. On the results screen, you'll see these suggested terms: design, illustration, tattoo, bathroom, wedding, architecture, jewelry, fashion, and many more. Keep scrolling to the right to see the rest of the terms.

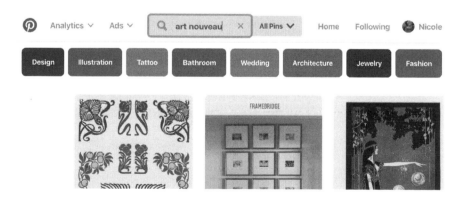

Let's say you selected **architecture**. On the results, you'll see more terms, such as houses, interior, furniture, stairs, buildings, Antoni Gaudi, drawings, steampunk, and more. Now select **buildings**, and on the results screen select **Paris France**. Now you have a good set of images for art nouveau buildings from Paris. Scrolling

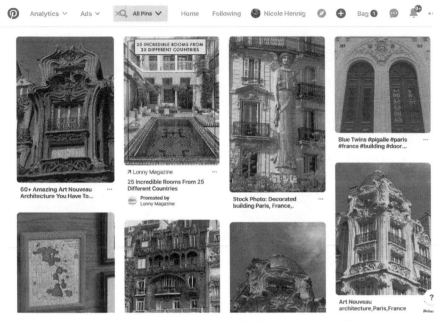

It's very useful to browse through visual results for visual topics like architectural styles.

through visual results is much more useful for a topic like this than clicking on text links from Google search results.

Clicking on a pinned image will bring you to a screen with more details. In most cases, people link the photo to its source on the web. If there is no link or other information about the source of the image, you could download it and do a reverse Google Images search, as described in Chapter 3. This may turn up the original source. But luckily, most images are linked to their source. You can easily save other people's pins into boards of your own, organized in ways that are useful to you. Each board you create can be set as public or private. This is a handy way to collect images with links to information for any sort of project.

Another useful feature is found in Pinterest's mobile app. Look for a camera icon in the search bar and tap it to take a photo of something. Pinterest will find images that look similar to objects in your photo. Pinterest promotes this mainly as a tool for shopping, but you can use it in other ways. It could be helpful if you want to find the name of an unknown object or tool, identify plants or animals, or find a product that looks similar to one you've seen.[8]

Remember that people can pin images from any website. So you'll find an amazing range of images on many topics. For example, try searching for **historical photos** and narrow it to **Victorian Era**. Costume designers use Pinterest for inspiration for the design of costumes for theatre productions. Try searching Pinterest for library displays, museum exhibitions, travel planning, lesson plans for teachers, recipes, interior design ideas, technology gadgets, and much more.

Chapter 5

Finding Old Websites

Using the Wayback Machine from Internet Archive

If you've ever wanted to search for an old version of a web page, Internet Archive's Wayback Machine is your tool. Find it at https://archive.org/web/. The Internet Archive[1] is a nonprofit dedicated to archiving websites and other digital artifacts. They have been archiving websites since 1996, and in 2001 they launched the Wayback Machine so anyone could search that archive. As of mid-2018, it contains over 334 billion web pages.[2] Their mission is to help preserve digital artifacts for researchers, historians, and scholars.[3]

To search the Wayback Machine, enter a specific URL in the search box at https://archive.org/web. This is not a full-text search engine, so don't enter keywords.[4] For an example, let's look at old versions of the New York Public Library home page, http://nypl.org. Start by entering **http://nypl.org** in the search box. On the results page, you'll see a timeline and a calendar. Select a date for the page you want to see. Keep in mind that not every date will have a result. It only saves pages on the days their crawler visits the page. As of July 23, 2018, the results screen for New York Public Library tells you that it was saved 5,114 times between January 3, 1997, and July 23, 2018.[5]

In the calendar view, look for a date with a blue dot on it. That indicates that the crawler received a good capture that day. Green indicates that a redirect was received, and other colors signify various other status codes. See https://archive.org/about/faqs.php#1278 for details about the meanings of these colors.

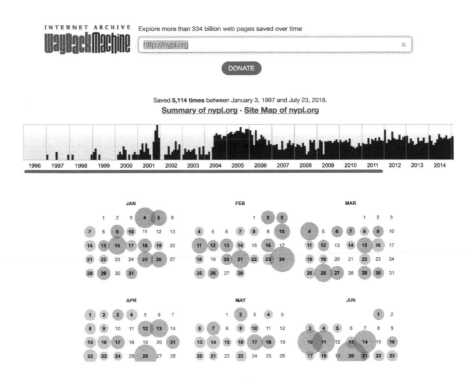

Use the timeline at the top to navigate to a specific year, such as 2009. On that year's page, click on a date with a blue dot, such as February 19.

There you will find a capture of the page on that day. It's common to see missing images on these pages, since their crawler may not have saved every single image on a page. You can use the timeline view on top of that captured page to navigate easily to other dates. If the page was made from dynamically generated content, it may not have been captured. (If a dynamically generated page outputs standard HTML, it can be captured, but some content from forms or JavaScript won't show up at all.)[6] You can follow links on pages in the archive and, if that page was also captured, it will bring you to that page on the same date. If not, the link might bring you to a current version of that page (if that URL still works), or to an error screen if the page wasn't captured.

One type of search that's interesting to do is to compare the same website 10 or 20 years ago and look at web design conventions from that time. If you go back to the first crawl of the New York Public Library, you'll see that it's dated January 3, 1997. As was common at that time, the page consisted of one large graphic with clickable regions, with the text links at the bottom of the page.

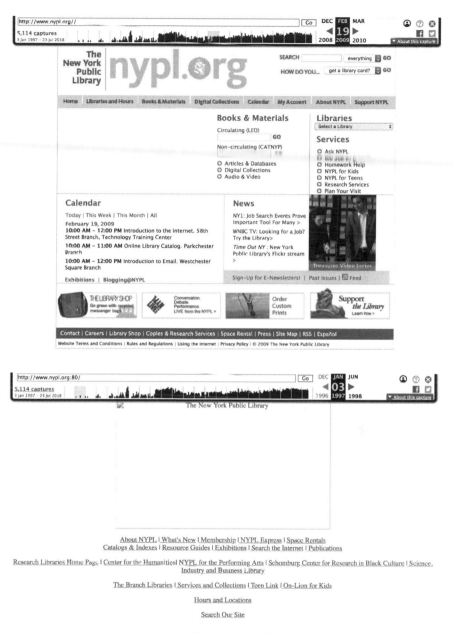

Images aren't always saved, as in this example where the whole site was one big image.

This capture is missing the image, but you can still click on the text links at the bottom.

If you want to make sure that a particular web page gets saved on a particular date, you can submit a link to the Wayback Machine.

Look for "Save Page Now" on the home page, and enter your link there. They also offer mobile apps for iOS and Android and browser extensions for Chrome, Firefox, and Safari. These apps and extensions are for the same purpose: submitting pages to the Wayback Machine to be saved. This has proven to be a useful way to find particular tweets that were later deleted, especially from well-known persons whose tweets are frequently saved by users in the Wayback Machine.[7]

Keep in mind that not every web page is archived by the Wayback Machine. They can't save sites that are password-protected or sites that block crawlers with a robots.txt file. If you don't want a page that you own to ever be saved by them, you can send an email request to info@archive.org.

Ways to Use the Wayback Machine

Here are a few ideas for using the Wayback Machine.

- Find an online manual for an obsolete product on old versions of the manufacturer's website.
- Look at old versions of your own website to see how it has changed over time.
- Research conspiracy theories. If you know of a particular site that has been taken down, you may still be able to find old copies of it.
- Find an ezine that is no longer being published if you know the URL of the old site.
- Compare historical prices to today's prices at a particular online store.
- Research the past of political candidates.
- Find news coverage of historic events, such as the events of September 11, 2001.
- Look at the history of internet search tools, such as AltaVista.com or Yahoo.com.

If you want to know more about the Wayback Machine, read their FAQ, found at https://archive.org/about/faqs.php#The_Wayback_Machine.

Using Google's Cache

If you ever want to find a *recent* previous version of a web page, Google's cache can come in handy. As Google crawls the web to store pages in its database for searching, it saves a temporary copy of each page in a place known as a cache. Searching this cache is useful in the following ways:

- See content that has been changed or deleted from a page.
- Access information from a site that is temporarily down or off-line permanently.
- Get past temporary blackouts like those used for protests.[8]

Not every page on the web is available this way. Some websites have a setting that instructs Google not to index old pages (by using a file called robots.txt). Also, websites can keep pages private by adding meta tags known as "noindex" and "nofollow." These instruct Google not to index the page (noindex) or not to index pages that are linked from a page (nofollow).[9]

Here's an example of how to search for pages in Google's cache. Let's say you are looking for a particular page on Wikipedia. You might enter **first law of thermodynamics wikipedia**. On the results screen, after the green URL under the title of your result, you will see a small down-pointing triangle. Click the triangle to see a menu from which you can select "cached."

At the top of the cached page, Google tells you the date and time of this version. It defaults to a full version, and you can switch to a text-only version by using the link at the top of the page. Some pages in the cache will not have the CSS style sheet applied, so it will look very different from the live page, but you can still read the page.

Another way to search for cached pages is to use a search operator, as in this example: **cache:chicago.suntimes.com**. Be sure not to leave a space after the colon.

About 660,000 results (0.59 seconds)

First law of thermodynamics - Wikipedia

https://en.wikipedia.org/wiki/First_law_of_thermodynamics ▼
This combined statement is the expression the **first law of therm**   reversibl
closed systems. This is one aspect of the **law** of conservation of   be state
energy of an isolated system remains constant.

| Cached |
| Similar |

History · Various statements of the ... · Evidence for the first law ... · First law of ...

This is Google's cache of https://en.wikipedia.org/wiki/First_law_of_thermodynamics. It is a snapshot of the page as it appeared on Aug 17, 2018 07:37:53 GMT. The current page could have changed in the meantime. Learn more.

Full version   Text-only version   View source

Tip: To quickly find your search term on this page, press **Ctrl+F** or **⌘-F** (Mac) and use the find bar.

👤 Not logged in Talk Contributions Create account Log in

Article   Talk   Read   View source   View history | Search Wikipedia   🔍 |

WIKIPEDIA
The Free Encyclopedia

First law of thermodynamics   🔒

From Wikipedia, the free encyclopedia

Main page
Contents
Featured content

The **first law of thermodynamics** is a version of the law of conservation of energy,

Thermodynamics

It can be very interesting to look at previous versions of pages that change often, such as newspaper sites, Wikipedia pages, specific Tweets, and so on. Google only keeps the most recent cached version and saves them for 24 hours, so if you are looking for older versions, use the Wayback Machine as described in the previous section.

Chapter 6

Data, Statistics, Comparisons

Using Wolfram Alpha

Wolfram Alpha is useful when you want to find data and statistics, solve math equations, do comparisons, and much more. It is known as a "computational knowledge engine," which means that it gives you specific answers to questions instead of possibly relevant websites (like Google does). It does this by searching its own internal database, which gets data from many sources.[1] The foundation for its math, engineering, and technical data is the company's flagship product, Mathematica, https://www.wolfram .com/mathematica, which covers algebra, symbolic and numerical computation, statistics, and data visualization. It gets other data from academic and commercial websites such as the CIA World Factbook, Chambers Biographical Dictionary, and the U.S. Geological Survey.

Wolfram Alpha is strongest in answering factual questions that rely on math calculations, data, and statistics. In addition to science and technology topics, it covers topics such as words and linguistics, history, arts and media, entertainment, hobbies, food and nutrition, and much more. A good way to get an idea of what's covered is to browse their examples page at https://www .wolframalpha.com/examples.

You can search it for free at https://www.wolframalpha.com. You can also use their mobile apps for iPhone, iPad, or Android found at https://products.wolframalpha.com/mobile. There are Pro versions available (see https://www.wolframalpha.com/pro/ pricing), but you can do so many things with the free version that I have never found a need for it. If it's something you use frequently, you might consider a subscription or site license.[2]

One of the most useful features of this tool is for comparing data. Let's say you want to compare data from three different 2017 hurricanes: Hurricane Harvey, Hurricane Irma, and Hurricane Maria. You can simply enter those three names into the search box. It's a natural language search engine, so you can also just type your query as you would speak it, such as **compare Hurricane Harvey, Hurricane Irma, and Hurricane Maria**. On the results screen, it will show you a note about any results it's assuming, with the option to click on different options, such as Harvey (1993) instead.

> **Assuming Harvey (2017) | Use Harvey (1993) or Harvey (1981) instead**
>   **Assuming Maria (2017) | Use Maria (2011) or Maria (2005) instead**

The answers are displayed in a handy table with a column for each hurricane. Rows include start and end dates, duration, maximum wind speed, and storm type (such as category 5 hurricane).

Below that is a map showing the path of each hurricane, coded by color. At the bottom, you'll find a list of sources for this data. Click "Sources" to open it, and click each item listed there to see the details about where this data came from.

As you can imagine, this is much more convenient than looking up each of these statistics one by one in Google. Try some other comparisons, such as the populations of various cities or countries, and salaries for various occupations—**salary of librarians in California vs Massachusetts**, for example.

Properties: [Show metric] [More]

	Harvey	Irma	Maria
start date	Thursday August 17, 2017 (11 months 18 days ago)	Sunday August 27, 2017 (11 months 8 days ago)	Saturday September 16, 2017 (10 months 19 days ago)
end date	Friday September 1, 2017	Tuesday September 12, 2017	Saturday September 30, 2017
duration	15 days	15 days	14 days
maximum wind speed	132 mph (August 26, 2017)	184 mph (September 7, 2017)	173 mph (September 20, 2017)
storm type	hurricane (category 4)	hurricane (category 5)	hurricane (category 5)

Units »

Storm path:

——— Harvey 2017   ——— Irma 2017   ——— Maria 2017

(track width indicates wind speed of storm)

📷 Sources   ⊕ Download Page   POWERED BY THE **WOLFRAM LANGUAGE**

Primary source: Wolfram|Alpha Knowledgebase, 2018

External source:

▸ *Tropical storm data*

▸ *Note*

Most people know Wolfram Alpha as a tool for math and science, but it's also useful for many other types of answers. One of the best is for word definitions. For example, enter **word**, followed by the word you want to look up, like this: **word actually**. The results include definitions, pronunciation, hyphenation, frequency, synonyms, rhymes, lexically close words, anagrams, translations (to several languages), use in movie titles, use in Internet domains, crossword puzzle clues, and Scrabble scores.

Overall typical frequency:

written: **652nd most common** (1 in 6803 words) (>99% adverb)

spoken: **103rd most common** (1 in 807 words)

Definitions »

(includes some inflected forms)

Word frequency history: [Linear scale ▼] [Binned ▼]

(from 1540 to 2008) (in occurrences per hundred thousand words per year)

Definitions »

Synonyms: [Show synonym network] [Meanings combined ▼]

really | in reality

Rhymes:

(none among common words)

To learn more about some interesting uses of this tool, see articles in the "Learning More" section of this book.

Chapter 7

Conclusion

Things to Remember

As you know, internet search tools are constantly changing, and it can be difficult to keep up with the particular details of each. The most useful way to approach this is to *not* think of these tools like library databases. With these tools, you often won't know the exact scope of the data you're searching. You probably won't use Boolean searching. You won't usually need or want to memorize specific search syntax. And don't expect your searches to be private unless you take specific steps, as I described in Chapter 1.

Instead, as I've discussed throughout this book, use these guidelines.

- Learn about and use the best sites for different types of searches.
- Find and use the search filters in each tool (which are often not apparent on the first screens).
- Since many tools these days use natural language searching (or something near it), don't expect precision when it comes to crafting a search query.
- Find out what you can about the scope of your tool. You may not be able to find out exactly what's included, as sometimes this is considered proprietary information.
- If there are specific commands you want to use in your search, check the help files of the search tool to make sure they haven't changed since you last used those commands.

- Go beyond Google. Search using other sites when you want to find images, videos, social media, comparison data, and old versions of web pages.
- Learn to protect the privacy of your searches.

There are many more useful search tools online that I haven't covered in this book. For a short guide like this, I needed to be selective. You can use the guidelines above no matter which internet search tools you use.

Ideas for Library Instruction

I hope you will find this short guide useful both for your own searching and for instruction you offer in your library. Feel free to use this book as a guide when creating your own instruction. Here are some ideas.

- Offer a series of workshops, each one based on particular chapters from this book.
- Create guides on your website about specific topics from this book. For example, see "Google Search Techniques: CEU Library," a guide I made for the library at Central European University in Budapest, Hungary: https://ceu.libguides.com/google-techniques.
- Create short instructional videos about specific topics, such as "How to Use Twitter Advanced Search" or "How to Find Old Web Pages Using the Wayback Machine."
- If you produce a library podcast, do shows about search tips like the ones in this book.

Resources—Learning More

Here are a few additional resources for learning more about some of the topics in this book.

Google

Maksimava, Masha. "Google's Personalized Search Explained: How Personalization Works, What It Means for SEO, and How to Make Sure It Doesn't Skew Your Ranking Reports." SEO Power Suite, August 22, 2017, https://www.link-assistant.com/news/personalized-search.html.

Google Maps

"The Coolest Places You Can Visit on Google Street View." Cool Material, accessed August 5, 2018, https://coolmaterial.com/cool -list/the-coolest-places-you-can-visit-on-google-street-view.

"Google Maps Treks." Google.com, accessed August 5, 2018, https://www.google.com/maps/about/treks.

Matchar, Emily. "The Rise of Indoor Navigation." Smithsonian .com, December 22, 2017, https://www.smithsonianmag.com/ innovation/rise-indoor-navigation-180967632.

Privacy Tools

Hennig, Nicole. "Privacy and Security Online: Best Practices for Cybersecurity." *Library Technology Reports* 54, no. 3 (April 2018). https://journals.ala.org/index.php/ltr/issue/view/677.

Twitter

Clark, Jon. "Everything You Need to Know About Twitter Advanced Search." Search Engine Journal, September 28, 2017, https://www.searchenginejournal.com/twitter-advanced-search -guide/214202.

Wolfram Alpha

"Examples for Surprises." Wolfram Alpha, accessed August 5, 2018, https://www.wolframalpha.com/examples/everyday-life/ surprises.

Collins, Jerri. "Things You Can Do With Wolfram Alpha." Lifewire, May 1, 2018, https://www.lifewire.com/wolfram-alpha -4035257.

Hoffman, Chris. "10 Amazing Uses for Wolfram Alpha." How-To Geek, February 29, 2012, https://www.howtogeek.com/106925/ 10-amazing-uses-for-wolfram-alpha

I hope you've found this short guide useful! I'd love to hear from you if you have ideas for future guides, or for updates to this one. Drop me a line using the form at http://nicolehennig.com/ contact-me, or email me at nic@hennigwcb.com. Thank you!

Notes

Chapter 1

1. "Search Using Autocomplete," Google Search Help, accessed June 16, 2018, https://support.google.com/websearch/answer/106230.

2. One exception to this is that you can turn off the inclusion of "trending stories." See Google's help for how to do this on Android or iOS mobile devices: "Search Using Autocomplete," Google Search Help, accessed June 16, 2018, https://support.google.com/websearch/answer/106230.

3. Kelly Marshall, "Google Instant—Why It Mattered and Why It Doesn't Anymore," IT Groove, July 27, 2017, http://itgroove.net/oh365eh/2017/07/27/2581/.

4. Learn more on Google's help page, "Filter Your Search Results," accessed June 16, 2018, https://support.google.com/websearch/answer/142143?hl=en.

5. Barry Schwartz, "Google Removes The + Search Command," Search Engine Land, October 24, 2011, https://searchengineland.com/google-sunsets-search-operator-98189.

6. Rebecca Sentance, "Everything You Need to Know About Natural Language Search," Search Engine Watch, April 12, 2016, https://searchenginewatch.com/2016/04/12/everything-you-need-to-know-about-natural-language-search-2/.

7. Collen Kriel, "Google Demonstrates Natural Language Processing and Context Improvements for Assistant at GDD Europe," Silicon Angle, September 8, 2017, https://siliconangle.com/blog/2017/09/08/google-demonstrates-natural-language-processing-context-improvements-assistant-gdd-europe/.

8. ICANN Archives, https://archive.icann.org/en/tlds/.

9. "What are the rules for registration of .biz, .com, .info, .name, .net, .org, and .pro names?" ICANN, accessed June 19, 2018, https://www.icann.org/resources/pages/faqs-84-2012-02-25-en#3.

10. It's especially important to use a VPN if you work with your laptop or mobile device on public Wi-Fi networks like coffee shops or airports. That's because it's easy for hackers to run tools that spy on all the traffic on a local network. If your data is encrypted with a VPN, the hackers won't be able to view it.

Chapter 2

1. Nick Ames, "Google Translate: The Unlikely World Cup Hero Breaking Barriers for Fans," *The Guardian*, July 11, 2018, https://www.theguardian.com/football/2018/jul/11/google-translate-world-cup-hero-fans-language-barriers.

2. Enrique Orduña-Malea et al., "About the Size of Google Scholar: Playing the Numbers," EC3 Working Papers 18, September 5, 2014, https://arxiv.org/abs/1407.6239v2.

3. Google, "Go Inside with Indoor Maps," accessed August 8, 2018, https://www.google.com/maps/about/partners/indoormaps/.

Chapter 3

1. See the license here, https://creativecommons.org/licenses/by/3.0.

2. See https://unsplash.com/license.

3. See https://unsplash.com/apps/ios

4. "Captioning—Using and Improving YouTube's Auto-Generated Captions," University of Colorado Boulder, Office of Information Technology, August 16, 2017, https://oit.colorado.edu/tutorial/captioning-using-and-improving-youtube%E2%80%99s-auto-generated-captions.

5. Learn more about Vimeo in this article by Justin Simon. "YouTube vs. Vimeo: What's the Difference?" TechSmith, May 15, 2018, https://www.techsmith.com/blog/youtube-vs-vimeo-whats-the-difference/.

Chapter 4

1. David Pierce, "Facebook Local Might Be the Only Facebook App You Need," *Wired*, November 10, 2017, https://www.wired.com/story/facebook-local-the-only-facebook-app-you-need/.

2. "The Top 20 Valuable Facebook Statistics—Updated July 2018," Zephoria Digital Marketing, https://zephoria.com/top-15-valuable-facebook-statistics/.

3. Berkman, Robert. *Find It Fast: Extracting Expert Information from Social Networks, Big Data, Tweets, and More* (p. 150). Information Today, Inc. Kindle Edition.

4. "Most Famous Social Network Sites Worldwide as of April 2018, Ranked by Number of Active Users (in Millions)," Statista, https://www.statista.com/statistics/272014/global-social-networks-ranked-by-number-of-users/.

5. See also Amy Mollett et al., *Communicating Your Research with Social Media: A Practical Guide to Using Blogs, Podcasts, Data Visualisations and Video*, Sage Publishing, 2017, https://us.sagepub.com/en-us/nam/communicating-your-research-with-social-media/book245914.

6. Instagram help page: "How Do I Search on Instagram?" https://help.instagram.com/1482378711987121.

7. Betsy Paton, "What's All the Interest in Pinterest? How Can It Be Used for Research Communication?" Research to Action, July 24, 2012, http://www.researchtoaction.org/2012/07/whats-all-the-interest-in-pinterest-how-can-it-be-used-for-academic-research-communication/.

8. Hillary Grigonis, "Pinterest's Expanded Visual Search Tools Help You Find Things You Can't Name," Digital Trends, November 14, 2017, https://www.digitaltrends.com/home/pinterest-visual-search-lens-updates-november-2017/.

Chapter 5

1. Learn more about the Internet Archive, https://archive.org/about/.

2. Learn more about how the Internet Archive defines web pages, websites, and web captures, https://blog.archive.org/2016/10/23/defining-web-pages-web-sites-and-web-captures/.

3. Internet Archive Frequently Asked Questions, https://archive.org/about/faqs.php#21.

4. It's possible they may add a full-text search in the future; see the FAQ, https://archive.org/about/faqs.php#The_Wayback_Machine.

5. https://web.archive.org/web/*/http://nypl.org, accessed July 23, 2018.

6. https://archive.org/about/faqs.php#11

7. Nancy Watzman, "TV News Record: Wayback Machine Saves Deleted Prez Tweets," Internet Archive Blogs, September 29, 2017, https://blog.archive.org/2017/09/29/waybackmachinesavedeletedpreztweets/.

8. Blackouts such as this one about net neutrality: Rhett Jones, "The Internet Blackout for Net Neutrality Is Coming and You Can Help," Gizmodo, December 11, 2017, https://gizmodo.com/the-internet-blackout-for-net-neutrality-is-coming-and-1821186037.

9. Lindsay Kolowich, "Using Noindex, Nofollow HTML Metatags: How to Tell Google Not to Index a Page in Search," HubSpot, accessed July 27, 2018, https://blog.hubspot.com/marketing/how-to-unindex-pages-from-search-engines.

Chapter 6

1. "Scope of Wolfram Alpha," Wolfram Alpha FAQ, accessed August 4, 2018, https://www.wolframalpha.com/faqs4.html.

2. Student and educator discounts are available here: https://www.wolframalpha.com/pro-for-students/ and https://www.wolframalpha.com/pro-for-educators/.

Index

About the Author

NICOLE HENNIG is an expert in emerging technologies for libraries. In her 14 years of experience at the MIT Libraries, first as web manager, then as head of user experience, she won awards for innovation, and worked to keep academics up to date with the best mobile technologies. In 2013 she left to start her own business helping librarians stay current with new technologies.

She is the author of several books, including *Keeping Up with Emerging Technologies: Best Practices for Information Professionals*. See her publications at http://nicolehennig.com/books, and online courses at http://nicolehennig.com/courses.

Nicole enjoys teaching, presenting, and inspiring people to use technology effectively. To stay current with the best new technologies, sign up for her email newsletter, Mobile Apps News, at http://nicolehennig.com.